ARNOLD

SCHWARZENEGGER

Biography

Being Useful in Life and Beyond

Kathryn M Schneider

CONTENTS

CHAPTER 1

HAVE A CLEAR VISION

So many of our best people have perished. So many of the good people have no idea what they're doing with their lives. They're bad for you. They are dissatisfied. Seventy percent of them are unhappy with their jobs. Their friendships are unsatisfying. They don't even crack a smile. They are not amused. They are completely exhausted. They are dissatisfied with their situation. They feel helpless, as if life is dragging them down a dead end road. These people can be found anywhere if you know where to search. Perhaps when you look in the mirror. It's OK. You are not damaged. They are neither. This is what happens when you don't have a clear goal for your life and settle for anything you can get or think you deserve. That is something we can work on. Because every good, every significant change begins with a clear vision.

The most critical aspect is vision. Vision is synonymous with meaning and purpose. To have a clear vision, you must have a clear picture of what you want your life to look like as well as a plan for getting there. People who are most dissatisfied with their lives have neither of these. They don't have a plan or a picture. They gaze in the mirror, puzzled, and wonder, "How the hell did I get here?" They've made so many decisions and taken so many acts to get here, and they have no idea what any of them were. They'll even fight with you, saying, "I hate this, why would I have chosen it?" Except no one pushed that ring on their finger or forced them to eat that second cheeseburger. Nobody forced them to take that dead-end job. Nobody forced them to leave class, work out, or attend church. Nobody forced them to stay up late every night playing video games instead of sleeping for eight hours. Nobody forced them to finish that final beer or spend their last dime.

Nonetheless, they truly believe what they are saying. And I believe they believe it as well. They have the impression that life has just happened to them. They truly believe they had no say over the course of their lives. And guess what? They are partially correct.

3

We have no control over where we come from. At the start of the Cold War, I grew up in a little village in Austria. My mother was quite caring. My father was severe and sometimes physically harsh, but I adored him. It was difficult. I'm sure your tale is also complicated. I'm sure growing up was more difficult than others around you believe. We can't undo the stories that have already been written, but we can pick where we go from there. There are causes and explanations for everything that has happened to us thus far, both good and bad. But it wasn't because we didn't have a choice, for the most part. We always have the option to choose. We don't always have something to compare our decisions to unless we make it. That is what a clear vision provides: a mechanism to determine whether a decision is good or bad for you based on whether it moves you closer or further away from your desired life path. Is the image you have in your head of your ideal future becoming blurrier or sharper as a result of what you're about to do?

The world's happiest and most successful people do everything in their ability to avoid making terrible decisions that muddle matters and lead them astray from their goals. Instead, they concentrate on making decisions that clarify their vision and get them closer to attaining it. The decision-making process is consistent regardless of whether they are considering a minor or major issue. The only difference between them and us, between me and you, between any two people, is the clarity of our vision for the future, the strength of our plan to get there, and whether or not we have recognized that the decision to make that vision a reality is solely ours. So, how do we go about doing that? How can we start from scratch with a clear vision? I believe there are two options. You can start small and work your way up until a big, clear picture emerges. Alternatively, you can start broad and then, like a camera lens, zoom in until a crisp image snaps into focus. That was my experience.

Start Broad and Zoom In

My first vision for my life was pretty broad. It was American. There is nothing more explicit than that. I was ten years old at the time. I'd just started high school in Graz, a large city to the east of where I grew up. In those days, it seemed like I was seeing fantastic things

4

about America everywhere I went. In my school courses, on magazine covers, and in newsreels that aired before movies at the theatre. There were photos of the Golden Gate Bridge and Cadillacs with enormous tail fins speeding down six-lane freeways. I watched Hollywood movies and rock 'n' roll stars on New York talk shows. I observed the Chrysler Building and the Empire State Building, which dwarfed Austria's tallest structure. Muscle Beach had streets dotted with palm trees and gorgeous girls. It was America in high definition. Everything was light and spacious. Those visuals were like Viagra for dreams for an impressionable kid like me. They should have also come with a warning, for the images of life in America they conjured up did not fade after four hours. This is where I belong, I knew.

What are you up to? I had no idea. As I have stated, it was a big vision. The image was pretty hazy. I was in my early twenties. What was I thinking? What I would discover is that some of the most powerful visions originate in this manner. From our passions when we were young, before our ideas about them were influenced by other people's opinions about them. When asked what to do when you're unhappy with your life, big wave surfer Garrett McNamara famously replied, "go back to when you were three, figure out what you loved doing, figure out how to make that your life, then make the road map and follow it." He was discussing the process of developing a vision, and I believe he is correct. It's clearly not that straightforward, but it might begin by going back in time and thinking widely about the things you used to enjoy. If you had paid attention to your passions in the beginning, they would have revealed your early vision for yourself. Consider Tiger Woods, who demonstrated his putting abilities on The Mike Douglas Show when he was just two years old. Or how about the Williams sisters? Many people are unaware that their father, Richard, introduced all five of his children to tennis when they were small, and they all excelled. Only Venus and Serena exhibited enthusiasm for the sport. Obsession. As a result, tennis became the framework for how they grew up and regarded themselves. Steven Spielberg experienced the same thing. When he was younger, he wasn't a huge moviegoer. He was a big TV fan. Then, for Father's Day one year, his father received a small 8mm home movie camera to document their family road vacations, and Steven began to experiment with it. Steven discovered filmmaking at the same age I was when I first learned about America. When he was twelve years old, he made his first film. When he was thirteen, he constructed one to obtain a photography merit badge in the Boy Scouts. He even brought the camera on Boy Scout outings. For Steven, who had recently relocated with his family from New Jersey to Arizona, filmmaking provided him with his first sense of purpose. It was not relocating to Hollywood. It wasn't winning Best Picture or Best Director at the Academy Awards. It wasn't having a lot of money or working with prominent people. Those more concrete goals would emerge later. His initial vision was simply to make movies. It was large and broad, just like Tiger's (golf), Venus and Serena's (tennis), and mine (America). This is quite normal. It's necessary for the majority of us. Anything more detailed becomes overly complicated and you get ahead of yourself. You begin to overlook critical roadblocks. When it comes to determining where and how to zoom in, having a broad vision gives you an easy, more accessible starting point. This does not imply that your vision becomes narrower, but rather more specific. The image becomes clearer. When you're attempting to plan a trip, it's like zooming in on a map of the world. The world is divided into continents. Countries exist within continents, states or provinces exist within countries, counties exist within counties, and cities and towns exist within cities and towns. And the point is, you can keep going like this indefinitely. Within towns, there are neighbourhoods, and within neighbourhoods, there are blocks. Streets connect individual blocks. If you're a tourist looking to explore the world, it doesn't matter if you go from nation to country or city to city. You do not need to pay close attention. But if you really want to get to know a city and make the most of your trip, if you might even want to call that area home someday, you should hit the streets, chat to residents, explore every back alley, understand the customs, and try new things. That is when the itinerary you are attempting to create—or the strategy you are attempting to construct in order to attain your vision—begins to take shape.

After the first clear picture of my future came into focus, my plan revolved around bodybuilding. When I was a teenager, I saw the current Mr. Universe, Reg Park, on the cover of one of Joe Weider's muscular magazines. That summer, I'd seen him play Hercules in Hercules and the Captive Women. Reg discovered bodybuilding as a poor child from a working-class area in England, then transitioned into acting after winning the Mr. Universe competition. That was my path to America, I realised right away. The journey and destination will be different for you. Maybe it's a professional shift and a change of environment. Maybe it's a hobby you want to convert into a way of life, or a cause you want to make your life's purpose. There truly isn't an incorrect answer as long as it sharpens your goal and clarifies the steps you need to take to attain it. Even individuals with the broadest of perspectives may find this phase tough. When I go to the gym these days, for example, I occasionally see someone strolling about, bouncing haphazardly from machine to machine like a Ping-Pong ball, with no apparent purpose for their workout. I'll approach this person and strike up a discussion. I've done this before, and it always ends the same way.

"What's your goal coming into the gym?" I'll inquire about them.

"To get in shape," they'll usually explain.

"Yes, great, fantastic, but get in shape for what?" I'll say it. This is a critical point because not all types of "in shape" are made equal. Being in bodybuilder shape will not help you if you want to be a rock climber. Carrying all that extra weight is going to injure you, not help you. Similarly, if you're a wrestler, being in shape like a long-distance runner is pointless since you need both raw strength and explosive quickness.

They'll pause, then stammer, looking for a response they believe I want to hear. But I don't let them off the hook by being silent. Most of them eventually give me an honest answer.

"My doctor said I need to lose twenty pounds and get my blood pressure under control."

"I just want to look good at the beach."

"I have young kids and want to be able to chase them around and wrestle with them."

These are all excellent responses. I can collaborate with any of them. Zooming in like that offers their vision some concentration, which will help them focus on the workouts that will help them achieve that goal. Bodybuilding is all about getting close. Not only should you focus on the specifics of your goals as a bodybuilder, but also on the actions you must take in the gym to get there. When I arrived in America as a twenty-one-year-old in the fall of 1968 and landed in Venice Beach to train at Gold's Gym under the great Joe Weider, I'd already won a number of titles in my professional debut, including Mr. Universe earlier that year. Those titles were stepping stones on the route that led me to Joe's attention and, finally, to America. However, they were not the final steps. Joe didn't pay for my trip to America because I was already a champion. He was investing in me because he believed I was more than a champion. By bodybuilding standards, I was still rather young. I also have a tremendous ambition to work hard and achieve greatness. Joe saw all of these qualities in me and thought I had a legitimate opportunity at becoming the greatest bodybuilder in the world, if not all time. And he was going to assist me in zooming in even more to truly understand what it takes to become the greatest ever. I was in America, Mr. Universe, and the work was just getting started.

Create Space and Time

Of course, not everyone develops a notion of what they want to accomplish with their lives by the age of fifteen, as I did. I was quite fortunate. I grew up in a rural village with dirt roads and no running water or indoor plumbing. I had nothing to do but imagine and let my imagination run wild. I was a blank canvas. Anything and everything has the potential to create an effect on me. That it did. Images of America. My pals and I were playing gladiators in the park. Reading a news article on a record-breaking powerlifter for school. Learning that one of my pals knew Mr. Austria, Kurt Marnul, and that he had trained in Graz. Watching Hercules and the Captive Women and discovering that Mr. Universe portrayed Hercules, and that Steve Reeves, who played Hercules before him, was also Mr. Universe. Then I came upon one of Joe Weider's muscle magazines, saw Reg on the cover, and discovered he was from a little working-class town just like me. All of these were inspirational moments that stayed with me. They worked together not only to construct the first vision I had, but also to refine and sharpen it, giving me something particular to work toward over the following twenty years.

For many people, discovering that kind of vision is a long-term process that takes years, if not decades. Some people never make it. They live in a world without vision. Not even memories of a childhood obsession that could have become a vision as an adult. The distraction of all our devices has squeezed out those memories and the possibilities they hold. They've been wiped out by everything that makes people feel helpless, as if life has happened to them. This is awful, but it is also utterly wrong to sit by and do nothing. To act as the victim. Nobody will construct the life you desire for yourself; no one will do it for you. It's okay if you don't know what that life looks like yet, for whatever reason. We've arrived. What is important is the decisions you make from now on. And there are two things you should do right now.

First, set little goals for yourself. Don't worry about the broader picture for the time being. Concentrate on making progress and saving accomplishments one day at a time. They can be fitness or nutrition objectives. They could be about networking, reading, or getting your house in order. Begin doing things you enjoy or that make you proud of yourself for completing. Do those activities every day with a little aim in mind, and then note how it alters what you pay attention to. You will find yourself looking at things in a new light. Create weekly and then monthly goals when you've established a routine with your daily goals. Instead of zooming in from a broad perspective, create your life from the ground up and let your vision expand from there. As it does, and the sensation of futility begins to fade, take the second step: put the machines away and make room and time in your life, however tiny or brief at first, for inspiration to enter and the discovery process to begin. I realise it's not as simple as it sounds. As you get older, your life becomes more busy and confusing. It can be difficult to find space and time without feeling like you're sacrificing some larger set of duties, especially now that you're crushing these little daily, weekly, and monthly goals. And, guess what, it's difficult at first. But do you know what's more difficult? Living a life you despise. That is difficult. By comparison, this is a piece of cake. Which it very well could be. Many of history's greatest philosophers, statesmen, scientists, artists, and entrepreneurs discovered inspiration while taking walks. Beethoven loved to go for walks with blank pages of sheet music and a pencil in his hand. William Wordsworth, a Romantic poet, used to write while walking around a lake near his home. Aristotle and other ancient Greek philosophers would educate their students while taking long walks with them, often hammering out their ideas at the same time. Two thousand years later, the philosopher Friedrich Nietzsche would observe, "It is only ideas gained from walking that have any worth." While wandering about the Princeton University campus, Einstein revised many of his theories about the universe. As Henry David Thoreau put it, "the moment my legs begin to move, my thoughts begin to flow."

Those are some really outstanding people who recognized the value of making time and space in their daily life to go for a stroll. However, walking does not require you to be a genius or a prodigy in order to be beneficial or transformative. There is a lot of evidence that going for a walk may boost creativity, inspire new ideas, and alter people's life, no matter who they are. A 2014 study conducted by Stanford University researchers found that walking boosted the creative thinking of all study participants who were instructed to walk while completing a series of creative tasks. There is also a lot of anecdotal evidence. If you do a fast Google search for the words "walk" and "change," you'll get a flood of stories with headlines like "How Taking a Walk Changed My Life." They're written by men and women, young and old, fit and unfit, students and professionals, Americans, Indians, Africans, Europeans, Asians, you name it. Going for a walk assisted them in changing their routines and habits; it assisted them in shaking loose answers to difficult situations; and it assisted them in processing trauma and making major life decisions. It did all of those things for an Australian named Jono Lineen. He intended to hike the full length of the western Himalayas—nearly seventeen hundred miles—by himself when he was thirty. The first person to do it alone. It was a challenge for him. He hiked for months, up to 25 miles each day, with nothing but his thoughts and the tremendously gorgeous Himalayas all around him. He couldn't get away from either of them. He eventually made a breakthrough.

He wasn't there to put himself to the test; he was there to fix himself. "I came to realise that what I was actually doing there in the mountains was coming to terms with the death of my younger brother," he wrote of his experience in a 2021 essay. He had struggled in the years following his brother's death. He had fallen into a rabbit hole of melancholy, and this simple yet arduous experience of walking across the Himalayas brought some clarity that lifted him out of it.

Years later, Jono had another life-changing experience, this time walking the 500-mile Camino de Santiago de Compostela, a famous Catholic pilgrimage across northern Spain. "I was trapped in a very stressful job in London and I needed a break," he told me. He'd decided to resign his work by the conclusion of the Camino, after nearly three weeks of walking over farms, through little towns, up and over mountains and valleys. "The change threw my life in a new and wonderful direction, and I'm thankful to walk for helping me achieve that."

Jono's story is not exceptional. Every year, over 300,000 people from all over the world walk the Camino, with less than a third of them doing so for religious reasons. The great majority of people have other motives. Reasons similar to Jono's. Reasons similar to yours, most likely. They're looking for inspiration, they're wanting to make a change, and what better way to find it than to go on a walk?

I've used the gym as a place to contemplate over the years. When I go skiing, I treat the ten or fifteen minutes in the chairlift as a hallowed space where I can let my thoughts roam. It's the same with bicycling. On a bike, no one can bother you, so you may let your thoughts wander wherever they may. I make room for ideas these days by taking a Jacuzzi every night. Something about the hot water and steam, the sound of the jets and the rush of the bubbles appeals to me. The sensation of floating, of not feeling the weight of my own body, sharpens all my other senses and opens me up to everything around me. The Jacuzzi provides me with 20 to 30 minutes of mental clarity. It's where I get some of my best ideas. I received the idea for my statement to the American people after the events of January 6, 2021 while sitting in the Jacuzzi. Like most people, I watched the rioting at the United States Capitol unfold on television and then in great detail on social media. And, like most people, I experienced a spectrum of feelings. Frustration. Disbelief. Confusion and rage. Finally, there is sadness. I was sad for our country since it had been a difficult day. But I also felt sorry for all the men and women, young and old, who were caught on camera as television networks chronicled the historic event and flashed their angry, desperate, and alienated expressions throughout the world. Whether they liked it or not, this was the imprint those people would leave on the world. This was going to be their legacy.

I thought about them a lot that night as I reclined in the Jacuzzi, letting the jets relax my strained neck and shoulder muscles from the day's stress. I gradually came to the conclusion that what we were all watching that day wasn't a political speech, it wasn't an attempt to refresh the tree of liberty with the blood of patriots and tyrants, as Thomas Jefferson might say... it was a scream for aid. And I wanted to assist them. That has been the focus of my life since 2003. Helping others. Volunteer work. Using the power that comes with celebrity and governmental office to improve the lives of as many people as possible. That was the direction my vision took for the third act of my life's film. But this was something new. Something extra. I was viewing all of these videos and reading real-time updates from folks who were there on Twitter and Instagram. Protesters. Police. Bystanders. Reporters. I reasoned that if they could reach me via social media, I could reach them as well. An image formed in my head quite rapidly. I imagined myself sitting behind my desk, holding the sword from Conan the Barbarian, delivering a speech that cut through all the crap between us, using my platform in ways I had never used before. That Sunday, I gave a statement on my Instagram account in the hope that by speaking directly to those who were suffering the most, I would be able to help them and possibly heal them. I shared my story. I spoke about America's promise. Then I raised the Conan sword, exactly as I had imagined a few days ago. I explained how, if we allow it, that sword could be a metaphor for our democracy. I explained that the harsher the conditions under which a sword is created—heating, beating, cooling, grinding, and so on—the stronger, sharper, and more resilient it becomes. I titled the speech "A Servant's Heart," not only because that's what we all needed to show to bring us through such a difficult period in our country's history, but also because I felt I owed it to the country. Since I was ten or eleven years old, I'd seen America as the world's number one country, the world's greatest democracy. America made all I had, everything I'd done, and the person I'd become possible. America is the only country on the earth where my vision could have become a reality. It was now under attack, and I wanted to protect it with a servant's heart. A "servant's heart" also represented the vision I was developing for how to use my social media presence to serve as many people as possible, all around the world, and in a far more direct way than ever before. It was the transformation of a twenty-year vision of public service into a new fourth act that would not have happened if I hadn't created a habit of making room every day for thinking and allowing inspiration and new ideas to come in. I don't care if you go for a stroll, go to the gym, read, ride your bike, or soak in a Jacuzzi. If you're stuck, if you're struggling to find a clear vision for the life you want, all I ask is that you set small goals for yourself to start building momentum, and that you set aside time and space every day to think, daydream, look around, be present in the world, and let inspiration and ideas in. Give what you're seeking for a chance to find you if you can't find it.

Really See It

When I say that I could imagine myself sitting behind the desk at my home office on January 6th, I really mean it. I could see it extremely clearly, like a movie in my head. That's how it's been my entire life, with every major goal I've had for myself. I could envision myself in America when I was a kid. I had no notion why I was there, but I was there nonetheless. I could feel the beach between my toes and the tropical sun on my skin. I could smell the water and hear the waves despite having never experienced either of these things before. The only time we saw waves was when we threw large pebbles into the deep water of the Thaler See, a man-made lake just outside of Graz, and watched the ripples roll outward. When I actually arrived in California, all of my impressions proved to be incorrect, some for the better and others for the worse (sand stinks), but the fact that I had such vivid impressions at all was a significant reason I came in the first place.

When I first fell in love with bodybuilding, I had no nebulous dreams of being a champion. I had a very precise concept of it, based on pictures of people like Reg Park celebrating his successes in bodybuilding mags. I could envision myself on the podium, carrying the winner's trophy. I could see the other contestants on the lower steps enviously, but also in amazement, looking up at me. I could see their clenched teeth and the colours of their posing briefs. The judges were rising and applauding. I could hear the crowd cheering and singing my name. "Arnold! Arnold! Arnold!" This was not a dream. This was a recollection that had not yet occurred. That's how it felt to me.

Before I landed my first leading part as an actor, I could see my name above the title on movie posters and theatre marquees, just like Clint Eastwood, John Wayne, Sean Connery, and Charles Bronson had their names above the titles of their movies, which I admired. Producers and casting directors were continually trying to get me to shorten my name to Arnold Strong or something else because they thought Schwarzenegger was too long. They complained that it was too long. What they didn't realize, but I could see for myself, was that Schwarzenegger looks fucking awesome in BIG letters above the title of a movie.

It was the same in politics. I'd had good experiences giving back to the community for years. In after-school programs, I worked with Special Olympics athletes and at-risk adolescents. In 1990, I was appointed chairman of the President's Council on Physical Fitness and Sports, and I travelled to all fifty states hosting fitness summits focused on getting our children more active. I was learning that I might have a large impact, and I began to consider how I might be able to help even more people, perhaps by entering politics.

The idea of running for office had been simmering for a long, but the vision for what that may entail remained hazy. The photograph was out of focus. Should I run for office in Congress? Want to become a mega-donor? Some people had expressed interest in running for mayor of Los Angeles, but who in their right mind would choose such a thankless job? I couldn't see anything. Then, in 2003, California Governor Gray Davis faced the potential of recall by California voters. The state was a total shambles. People and companies were departing. There were intermittent blackouts. Taxes were out of control. Every week, there was another report about horrible news in California, and each week, I grew angry, hoping that this recall election would happen. When it became evident that it would proceed, the picture came into sharp focus. I imagined myself sitting behind the governor's desk in Sacramento, meeting with Democratic Assembly members, doing the people's business, and getting California back on track. I planned to run, and I planned to win.

My mental image was so clear that it could have been framed and hung on a wall. In that way, it was eerily similar to my vision for January 2021. I could make out the desk. What was on the desk was visible to me. I was able to see what I was wearing. I could see where the cameras would be placed and where the lights would be placed. The Conan sword was visible and felt in my hands. I could hear my voice rising and falling as I addressed the major issues we faced and presented my answers.

Before I go any further, I realise this seems like a lot of woo-woo manifestation mumbo jumbo, similar to The Secret and all those law of attraction books peddled by charlatans. This is not it. I'm not arguing that if you simply picture what you desire, it will come true. No way, no how. You must plan, work, learn, and fail, and then plan, work, and fail some more. That's just the way it is. Those are the guidelines. What I mean is that if you want your vision to stick, if you want your success to look exactly like you hoped it would when you first decided what you wanted your life to look like, you need to get crystal clear on that vision and tattoo it to the inside of your eyelids. You must SEE IT.

Elite athletes are aware of this. They are experts at picturing their objectives. In fact, visualising has been the difference between decent and exceptional players at practically every major international sport's highest level. Michael Phelps, the Olympic swimmer, was famed as a youngster for picturing his split timings down to the tenth of a second during training and hitting them lap after lap. Jason Day, an Australian golfer, takes a step back behind his ball, closes his eyes, and visualises his approach—from his address, to his backswing, all the way through contact, and envisioning the ball going where he wants it to. Sebastian Vettel, the German Formula One driver, was notorious for sitting in his car before qualifying sessions with his eyes closed, envisioning every corner, gear shift, acceleration and braking zone during his several world championship seasons. Almost every driver on the Formula One grid can now close their eyes, extend their hands out in front of them as if gripping a driving wheel, and take you on a hot lap of the circuits they visit each season.

They do this because doing what they do at a high level is really difficult. It requires an unbelievable amount of effort, skill, and practice just to get into the elite ranks and be competitive. More than simply ability and passion are required to win. You can't just put yourself into the winner's circle. You must be able to see your way there. When most elite MMA fighters train, they will rise up and circle the mat with their arms raised in victory at the finish of a three- or five-round sparring session. They are imagining how their next fight will turn out. "What you can see,you can 'be," as sports psychologist Don Macpherson memorably stated. You must be able to visualise what you want to achieve before you begin, not after you begin. That is the distinction.

As crucial as knowing what success looks like is understanding what it does not look like. There are a lot of things in this world that will get you a knockoff version of your ambitions, but will ultimately throw you off course if your mental picture of your life is even somewhat hazy. Knowing what is and isn't success gives your vision crystal clarity. And, I've discovered, with that clarity comes a sense of serenity, because practically every question becomes easy to answer.

After winning my fifth Mr. Olympia title in a row in 1974, I received a phone call from the original fitness pioneer, Jack LaLanne. Jack designed several exercise machines and the notion of health clubs. He had about 200 clubs at the time and wanted me to be their spokesperson. I'd be a sort of fitness ambassador, conducting promotional tours and ads. They offered me $200,000 each year. In 1974, that was a lot of money. It's still a large sum of money. Back then, the top bodybuilders in the world made no more than $50,000 per year. It was an incredible offer. And I turned it down without hesitation.

Being a national spokesperson for a health club franchise was not in my plans. I didn't think it was shameful or beneath me in any way. Anyone who cared about physical fitness saw Jack LaLanne as a hero. The issue was that accepting his offer would preclude me from working in movies, which was where my vision was guiding me at this time in my bodybuilding career. Knowing that made it much easier to say no. I was fine with passing up all that money and the different kinds of celebrity that the job would offer. I felt cool, knowing that I'd just passed up a fantastic opportunity but also a major distraction.

If you can't see your goal clearly—if you can't imagine what success is and isn't—it's difficult to appraise possibilities and difficulties like these. It's nearly hard to predict whether they'll bring you what you want or something close, and whether "close" is good enough for you. Having a clear mental picture can help you determine whether the thing you're going to do, the decision before you, is the difference between ordering Coke and getting Pepsi, or between taking your dream vacation to Hawaii and landing in Guam. They're both on the Pacific, have nice weather, and use the same currency, but only one has a Four Seasons.

Sports are far less forgiving. Settling for something close to your goal, anything in the ballpark, can mean the difference between winning and losing. Nobody enters athletics expecting to lose. So why would you go through life not aiming for what you truly desire? This is not a dress rehearsal, practice, or training session; it is the real deal. It's the only one you've got. So look at it... and then be it.

Look in the Mirror

When you look in the mirror, what do you see? Is there a winner or a loser? Is it someone who is joyful or someone who is unhappy?

Someone with vision or someone who has lost their way? Here's a simpler question: what colour are your eyes? And don't tell me they're blue, brown, or anything else. That is nonsense for your driver's licence. What exactly hue are they?

Isn't it complicated?

Many people struggle with these questions. The majority of individuals despite gazing in the mirror. They virtually seldom look themselves in the eyes when they do. It's really too unpleasant. It's too frightening. Because the person in the mirror is frequently a stranger who looks nothing like the person they see when they close their eyes and imagine themselves as.

As unpleasant as it may be, you must examine yourself in the mirror every day in order to know where you stand. You must check in with yourself to ensure that you are headed in the right way. You must ensure that the person looking back at you is the same as the person you see when you close your eyes and picture the person you want to be. You must determine whether your vision corresponds to the reality of your options.

Obviously, you must do this to avoid being lost and worthless. However, you must do it in order to avoid becoming a nasty person. Amazing people may be found in the fitness industry, Hollywood, and politics, in my experience. I've met a lot of them. They're also full of jerks, jerks, and assholes. I've met a number of them as well. Each one is worse than the last. Wait until you meet a studio executive with a lot of money and no taste, or a politician who believes the world revolves around them because forty thousand people voted for them in some remote corner of your state. Trying to go through the nasty sections of these worlds was like trying to move through a collection of Russian nesting dolls filled with excrement and hair gel. And the issue is, if you're not sure of yourself or what you're trying to do, it's extremely easy to get eaten up by them.

The distinction between the excellent and terrible is straightforward: self-awareness and clarity of vision. The good ones know exactly what they want to accomplish and are rigorous in judging their choices against that vision. They often check in with themselves.

Their perception shifts as they do. It grows and evolves alongside them. The good ones aren't afraid of looking in the mirror.

The terrible ones avoid looking in the mirror like the plague. Many of them lost their vision a long time ago, and as a result, the most shallow, self-centred form of the vision grabbed them and dragged them along for the ride. They never clarified their ambitions or zoomed in on what their world may look like in real life if they achieved it. They never felt compelled to. These are the people that entered into finance because they only wanted to be wealthy. They went to Hollywood in order to become famous. They entered politics because they desired power. And their vision never grew any deeper or wider than that because the earliest, broadest form of it served them well. They'd achieved success in the one area that had initially mattered to them, and hey, if it ain't broke, don't repair it, right? Even when it isn't working for everyone else.

I've spent my entire adult life staring at myself in the mirror. As a public servant and philanthropist for the past two decades, the mirror has taken the form of votes, polling numbers, statistics, and data. There is no ignoring the numbers as governor of California, head of the President's Council on Physical Fitness and Sports, and climate warrior. The people will show you what they think of you and your ideas through their comments, votes, and actions. They will tell you if they believe you or believe in you. When the data comes in and the needle moves, you can tell whether your vision is true or a delusion.

In Hollywood twenty years before that, the mirror was the camera and the movie screen. Whatever image I had for the film performance I wanted to give pales in contrast to what five hundred people sitting in the dark witnessed when I was thirty feet tall on the screen in front of them. The camera does not deceive. It shoots in high definition, in full focus, at 24 frames per second. I was only onscreen for twenty-one minutes in The Terminator, but that's more than thirty thousand individual photos saved forever. What I believed I was accomplishing in those sequences was only important if the audience saw it as well. Only then could I call myself a success. Only then could I declare that my vision as an actor had been realised in that picture. As a bodybuilder, the mirror was a literal mirror for the previous twenty years. Every day, I looked in the mirror. For several hours. It was a necessary aspect of the work. The mirror was an indispensable instrument. You can't tell if an exercise is effective unless you observe yourself doing it in the mirror. You can't tell if a muscle has enough mass or definition unless you flex it in the mirror. You won't know if you've mastered all of your motions until you stand in front of the mirror and do each posture one after the other.

Franco Columbu and I are in a ballet classroom in New York City studying movement from a ballet instructor in the opening scene of Pumping Iron. We're working on improving our posing skills. She changes our body positions, altering our posture and eyeliner, and smoothing out our transitions to make everything look more fluid and spectacular. She made an excellent point when working with us about paying attention to how we moved between postures. Onstage, the judges aren't simply looking at you while you're fully flexed and performing at your best. "What you have to realise," she added, "is that people are watching you all the time." She was completely correct! Static stances may be what end up in magazine images. They could be how people who weren't present learn about you. However, the individuals in the room, the people who matter, will be monitoring and judging every movement and transition between those important moments. It was an excellent metaphor. Life isn't simply about the highs and lows. It's not just the things that get burned into people's memories or captured in images that wind up in scrapbooks. Life is also defined by the gaps in time. Life happens in the transitions just as much as it does in the poses. It's all one lengthy performance, and the more impactful you want that performance to be, the more crucial each of those small moments becomes.

The other two walls of the instructor's studio are nothing but mirrors, which you don't see due to the camera angle in the first scene. Dancers, like bodybuilders, are aware. You can't improve unless you observe yourself doing the work. You can't improve unless you compare your efforts to what you know they should be in your heart and head. To give a performance of a lifetime, to attain any kind of vision, no matter how ridiculous or impossible, you must be able to see what the rest of the world sees as they watch you try. That does not imply conforming to the expectations of the world; rather, it means not being frightened to stand in front of the mirror, look oneself in the eyes, and truly perceive.

CHAPTER 2

NEVER THINK SMALL

By the end of 1987, I'd killed 283 people. More than anyone else in Hollywood during that time, by far. It took me eight films, but I did it. And that meant something. It meant that I was an action movie star. My name was above the title of most of my films. In big block letters just like I'd envisioned:

SCHWARZENEGGER

I'd done it. That's exactly what everyone said. Journalists. Executives from the studio. Agents. My associates. They spoke to me as if the job was done. It seemed as if there was nothing left for me to prove. "So, what's next for Arnold?" they'd ask, astounded by how far I'd come and unable to believe there was anything further to do. They were thinking on a tiny scale. My objectives had shifted. They were constantly developing. Another, larger picture had become clear to me. I didn't only want to be a top-billed action star. I aspired to be a leader. I aspired to be the highest-paid actor in the industry. To do so, I needed to demonstrate to everyone that I was more than just muscles and mayhem. I needed to show them my sensitive side, my dramatic side, my hilarious side, and my human side. I had no choice except to do comedies. This was not believed to be a good idea by anyone. Journalists believed I'd be useless. Executives at the studio did not believe audiences would accept it. My agents predicted that I would have to take a pay cut. Some of my friends worried I'd make a fool of myself. I respectfully disagree.

I'd met the wonderful comedy producer and filmmaker Ivan Reitman a year previously. I told him about my vision and what I hoped to accomplish. He'd seen all of the other aspects of me that I was now eager to show the rest of the world. And he was aware of it. He saw what I saw as I imagined the next stage in my path. Ivan also recognized that the Hollywood system is rife with sceptics. Because it was the easiest thing for them to understand, their impulse would be to keep me in my lane. Send scripts for additional action movies to Arnold, who is an action star. I couldn't approach a group of executives and request that they consider me for their next big studio comedy. If I wanted to be in a comedy, I'd have to pitch the idea to them and make it impossible for them to say no. That's exactly what we did. Ivan had a couple of writer buddies come up with some concepts, which Ivan and I worked on until we found one that we both liked and thought the studios would adore.

Twins grew from that concept. A buddy comedy about twin brothers Julius and Vincent, who were created in a lab and separated at birth, only to reunite 35 years later. I'd be Julius, the "perfect" one. Danny DeVito would play Vincent, a petty criminal whom Julius bails out of jail when they first meet.

We worked well together. I'd just gotten back from Commando and Predator. After five seasons on Taxi, Danny had recently completed the Romancing the Stone films. And Ivan had just finished directing Ghostbusters. Who wouldn't want to collaborate on a humorous film with us?

As it turns out, the majority of Hollywood. Everyone loved the premise, but some studio executives couldn't get past the fact that I was playing a comedy lead. They didn't think I could compete with Danny, who was a comic genius. Others thought I couldn't pull it off no matter who played opposite me. Then there were many who grasped the concept and saw the hilarious potential of our collaboration, but couldn't stomach the price tag when set against the likelihood of failure. We were all at the peak of our game, and we didn't come cheap. If the studio gave us our going rate, the film would be prohibitively expensive to produce, and it would have to do more than just succeed in order for them to make the type of profit they desired.

Ivan, Danny, and I collaborated to devise a strategy. We loved the story and were certain that if a studio gave us the money to create the film, it would be a success. We only needed to convert one sceptic into a believer. Our idea was to take no up-front money to decrease the studio's risk as much as feasible. If a studio agreed to make our film, all three of us would agree to work for free. Instead, we would take a cut of the net profits, known as the "backend" in Hollywood parlance. We would only profit if the studio profited. We realised

23

that we were attempting a significant feat. Back then, studios practically never provided actors' backend. (This is still the case.) With this initiative, each of us faced significant professional risk. There was also financial danger in postponing our remuneration. But we decided that if we were going to do it, we should do it right. We found our believer in Tom Pollock, the president of Universal. Just as Ivan saw in me what I saw in myself as a leading man, Tom saw in the Twins what we saw in them. If you can believe it, he even tried to persuade us to pay up front! But we stayed firm and committed to the original plan that got us here, and Tom gave us what we asked for.

We were in production in Santa Fe, New Mexico, by early 1988. By early 1989, we'd not only had a presidential screening at the Kennedy Center for President-Elect George H. W. Bush, but we'd also crossed the $100 million mark in domestic box office, making it my first film to do so. People still don't believe me when I tell them that Twins is the film that made me the most money in my whole career.

Ignore the Naysayers

There will always be people in your life who are sceptical of you and your dreams. They will say it is impossible. That you can't do it or that it's impossible to do. The bigger your dream, the more frequently this will occur, and the more of these people you will encounter. Throughout history, some of our greatest performers and creative minds have had to cope with those who didn't understand. The Lord of the Flies author was rejected by publishers 21 times. The first Harry Potter novel, written by J. K. Rowling was rejected 12 times. Todd McFarlane, the legendary comic-book artist, was rejected 350 times by various comic-book publishers. Andy Warhol donated one of his drawings to the Museum of Modern Art for free, and they returned it! Francis Ford Coppola was dismissed many times by the producers of The Godfather because they didn't believe his version of the story. Both U2 and Madonna were rejected by many record labels before signing deals.

In the business world, it's the same story. When the founders of Airbnb first tried to raise funds, they were turned down by all seven investors they approached. Steve Jobs was let go by his own corporation. Walt Disney's first animation company failed. Netflix wanted to sell to Blockbuster for $50 million, but they were laughed out of the room. Jack Ma, the founder of Alibaba, was rejected from Harvard ten times and couldn't even find a job at Kentucky Fried Chicken at one point. Almost every major technological achievement of the twentieth century was criticised at some point by someone who "knew better" for being silly, impractical, or just plain stupid. One critic wrote to Arthur Jones, the developer of the Nautilus workout machine, saying, "You want to have constant and uniform muscular development throughout all of your muscles? It's impossible. It's simply a fact of life."

The one thing all of these remarkable people have in common is that they persisted in the face of doubt and mistrust. There will always be sceptics. That doesn't give them the right to interfere in your life. They aren't necessarily bad people. They're simply ineffective for someone like you. They are terrified of the unfamiliar and unknown. They are hesitant to take chances and put themselves out there. They've never had the guts to do what you're doing. They've never created a grand vision for the life they want and then devised a strategy to make it a reality. They've never put everything on the line. Do you want to know how I know this? Because they would never tell you to give up or that it is impossible. No, they would have encouraged you in the same way I am today!

The doubters have no idea what they're talking about when it comes to you and your aspirations. And if they haven't done any of the things you're attempting to do, you should ask yourself, "Why should I ever listen to them?"

You shouldn't, is the response. You should disregard them. Or, even better, listen to what they have to say and then use it as motivation. As I approached my final Mr. Olympia competition in 1975, I conducted numerous interviews with journalists from various muscle and fitness magazines, as well as larger media agencies. They all wanted to know why I was leaving bodybuilding and what I was going to do next. I said the same thing to all of them. I was honest with them. In the sport of bodybuilding, I had attained everything I had ever desired and more. I didn't get the same type of joy from winning bodybuilding prizes as I used to, and it was all about the joy for me. I was looking for a new challenge. I informed them I was going to start advertising bodybuilding competitions instead. And I was planning on becoming a leading man in the performing world. I can count on one hand the number of journalists who listened to me outline my acting aspirations and said, ten years later, "You know what, I can see it." Only a few people mentioned something like that. The remainder either sneered and rolled their eyes or laughed out loud. Even some of the others standing about watching, such as photographers and camera operators, laughed. You can hear it on some of the remaining footage of those interviews.

But I didn't become upset. I welcomed their reservations. When I told them I wanted to be an actress, I expected them to scoff. It gave me energy. It was exactly what I needed. There are two explanations for this.

First and foremost, breaking into acting is difficult regardless of who you are. With my background, the way I wanted to do it would be exceedingly difficult. I didn't want to be simply another character actor driving around Los Angeles every day going to auditions for roles with a few lines here and there. I aspired to be the next Reg Park, playing iconic parts such as Hercules, or the next Charles Bronson, portraying an action hero who takes out bad men. Initially, I would meet with casting directors and producers. They'd listen to my description of what I wanted to accomplish, then tell me I could play a tough man, a bouncer, or a soldier. They'd remark things like, "War movies always need Nazi officers!" as if I should be happy or content with it. One of the guys at Gold's who was a TV stuntman said, "I can get you a job on Hogan's Heroes right now!" I recall one of the first times I voiced my ambition to act, maybe before I'd even won my first Mr. Olympia. On top of all the hard work required to become a good actor—acting classes, improv classes, language and speech classes, dance classes—I was going to need all the motivation I could muster to overcome the opposition of these sceptics who held positions of power or influence and stood in my way.

Second, I wanted their scepticism and laughter because it worked for me. Growing up in Austria, negative reinforcement was used in all sorts of motivation. From the early days of infancy, everything has been negative. When I was a kid, one of the most popular books of German fairy stories was called Der Struwwelpeter. It features eleven stories on how disobedient children can ruin everyone's lives with tragic results. When St. Nicholas comes to your house at Christmas to offer gifts to all the good boys and girls, he is accompanied by Krampus, a demon-like monster with large horns whose mission it is to punish all the evil kids and scare them straight. On the Feast of St. Nicholas, dads in small communities like That would go to each other's houses wearing Krampus masks and scare the snot out of each other's kids. Our downstairs neighbour was my Krampus. My father served as the Krampus for several families in the village.

Krampus and Der Struwwelpeter performed admirably. They kept the children in line. However, for a subset of people who were wired differently, negative reinforcement produced something else: motivation. The goal is not to "be good," but to get out. To escape, to progress to bigger and better things. I was one of those kids who had a strange wiring. Since then, I've transformed any negative energy hurled at me into inspiration. Telling me it can't be done is the quickest method to persuade me to bench press 500 pounds. The simplest method to ensure that I become a movie star was for you to laugh when I told you about my idea and then tell me I couldn't accomplish it.

You have a choice when it comes to the naysayers on your path to success. You can ignore them or use them, but you can never believe them.

No Plan Bs

When I became governor of California in 2003, I inherited a slew of detractors in the form of the California State Legislature. Democratic members didn't want to hear what I had to say since I was a Republican who wanted the state to live within its means rather than spend the money of future generations. Republicans did not trust me because of my views on the environment, gun control, and health-care reform. It was a difficult scenario to enter, but I had no choice but to disregard it. I had to ignore their opposition to my views. My objective was to find a way to work with them all in order to pass legislation that would benefit the people of California. That means making a concession. I would work with the legislature on measures whose aims we could agree on wherever we could find common ground, as long as I didn't feel like we were letting people down or making their lives more difficult. Leaders in Sacramento gradually realised that I was a reasonable and thoughtful individual. I wasn't a partisan hack; I was honest. We could collaborate. But, over those first few years of trying to get things done, there was always a moment at the end of meetings that gradually brought a new vision for my work as governor into view. It would work like this: my team and I would meet with a legislator to discuss a bill I was proposing. I would explain how much it would cost, how it would benefit the people in their district, and how grateful I would be if they would support me. They'd say things like, "We've needed to do something like this for a long time," and they'd agree it'd be good for their constituency. And that's when it happened. They'd lean back in their chair, saying, "I love it... but I can't bring this back to my district."

I had no idea what they were talking about because I was new to this type of politics. What do you mean you won't be able to return it to your district? Get on a plane, return to your district, sit in your office, and meet with your constituents to explain what we're trying to accomplish here in Sacramento. If I bring this back to my constituents, they will say that I am going to lose my next election to someone from my own party because my support for this law proves that I am either too liberal or too conservative. They'd argue I'm in a "safe seat," and by supporting this law, I'd be making the seat unsafe... for me. They were discussing the consequences of hailing from a gerrymandered area. I was astounded to discover about the extent of gerrymandering, not just in California, but across the country and at every level. And that it has been going on for the past two centuries! When it became evident to me that one of the major reasons no-deal legislation was being passed was because electoral districts were being designed every ten years by the same politicians who would gain from revised boundaries, I knew we needed to fix these maps right now. As governor, it became a major priority for me. Based on the reaction of people from both parties when I submitted a redistricting reform proposal to the ballot in 2005, you'd think I was trying to take away their free supply of American flag lapel pins. It made no one happy. Many lawmakers were enraged. Everyone told me it couldn't be done, that it wouldn't happen, that I couldn't do it.

That was their first blunder. When they triumphed in 2005 and the redistricting initiative was defeated at the polls, they said that was the end of the matter. They expected me to give up and move on to something else, to a different set of objectives. This was their second blunder. When an issue like redistricting reform comes into sharp focus in my mind, when it becomes a personal objective for me, I don't let it go. I'm not going anywhere. I won't give up. And I don't make any concessions. There is no backup plan. Plan B is to be successful with Plan A.

That is exactly what occurred.

I brought it up several times during the next three years. I spoke with everyone who was open to having an open and honest discussion about gerrymandering. I sought input from all parties on the best way to effect genuine change. All of that effort was included into a new redistricting reform legislation for the 2008 election, which was considerably more aggressive than the one I proposed in 2005. That one was defeated by 19 percentage points. This one received nearly double the number of votes as the previous one. In three years, we had nearly doubled voter support for redistricting reform and given the people the ability to determine election maps.

This is what may happen when you set lofty goals. When you put everything on the line. When you disregard the critics. When you stick to your principles. Good things can happen for you and everyone you care about on a scale that others never imagined imaginable.

Let me tell you a story: Having a backup plan has never resulted in anything positive. Nothing significant or life-changing, in any case. Every grandiose idea is jeopardised by Plan B. It's a doomed strategy. Plan B is the path of least resistance if plan A is the road less travelled, if you're creating your own way toward the goal you've built for your life. And once you know that road exists, once you've accepted that it's an option, it's so much easier to choose it when things become tough. Plan B is a shambles! When you make a backup plan, you not only give all the doubters a voice, but you also limit your own dream by admitting the reality of their concerns. Worse, you become your own sceptic. There are already enough of them; you don't need to add to their numbers.

Break Records and Blaze Trails

There is a legend concerning Sir Edmund Hillary, the first person to reach the summit of Mount Everest. When he returned to base camp, he was greeted by the media who inquired about the view from the top of the globe. He described it as extraordinary because, while he was up there, he noticed another mountain in the Himalayan range that he hadn't yet climbed, and he was already planning his route to conquer that peak next. When you reach the summit, you gain a completely different perspective on the rest of the world and your life. You notice new obstacles that were previously invisible, and you notice old challenges in new ways. With this massive triumph under your belt, they all become manageable. Hillary ascended other unclimbed summits after Everest, including the one he told reporters about. Following the success of The Terminator and Predator, I ventured into comedy with Twins and Kindergarten Cop, both of which were the biggest films I'd ever done when they were released. Michelangelo did not stop producing after sculpting his David; he painted the ceiling of the Sistine Chapel, one of the great masterworks of the Italian Renaissance. Elon Musk did not take his money and leave after confounding PayPal and inventing internet banking. He started SpaceX, which changed space travel, and subsequently joined Tesla, which revolutionised electric vehicles.

Fulfilling a dream empowers you to look further and deeper—further out into the world toward what is possible, and deeper within yourself toward what you are capable of. That is why there are so few stories about people who have accomplished great things and then simply packed their belongings and relocated to a private island, never to be heard from again. People that think large and succeed virtually always keep pushing, striving, and dreaming bigger. Consider the last time you accomplished something challenging that

30

you were proud of. Did you stop doing anything after that? Obviously not. This success provided you the confidence to try new things. Something new. All the greats are like this. They may not succeed at their highest degree of achievement. One-hit wonders abound in the music industry. There have been many writers who only wrote one outstanding book or directors who only directed one amazing film. They never stop working or dreaming, however. They never say things like, "I made it, my work here is done." They will work to achieve the vision they have set for the life they wish to live for the rest of their lives.

Thinking big and succeeding has an effect on us. It surely had an effect on me. It got addicted because I discovered that the only true restrictions reside in our brains. I understood that our potential— mine and yours—is boundless! What's equally amazing, I believe, is that other people understand their own potential is boundless when they see someone like you or me break down barriers and forge new paths. When we imagine large and make our own goals come true, those dreams come true for others as well.

Before Sir Edmund Hillary and his sherpa, Tenzing Norgay, reached the summit of Everest on May 29, 1953, there had been nine failed missions. Four Swiss climbers would follow suit within three years. More than 200 climbers would reach the peak of Everest in 32 years, the same amount of time it took to complete the first successful ascent. A Canadian weightlifter called Doug Hepburn became the first person to bench-press 500 pounds the day before Hillary reached the summit. For many years, 500 was considered a magical number for the bench press. Bruno Sammartino would break Hepburn's record with a 565-pound lift by the end of the decade. I've benched 525 pounds on my own. The unassisted record is now well over 750 pounds, having been broken and unbroken countless times since.

I've witnessed this process in my own life. Nobody ever left Austria before I arrived in America. Perhaps you went to Germany to work in a factory. If you were feeling very daring, you might relocate to London to work in business. But what about America? No way. After I won all those Mr. Olympia competitions and then did the

Conan movies, I started seeing Austrians and Germans all over Los Angeles. They'd come to get into the fitness industry, Hollywood, and all the other things they'd read about me accomplishing in the same magazines I'd read about Reg Park in years before. I'd opened the door to America for them without even wanting to, and to their credit, these men and women went through it.

It's really inspiring to see someone with a crazy aim give it everything they've got and then succeed. It's like magic because it reveals potential we didn't even realise we have. It demonstrates what is possible when we set our minds to something and then put up the necessary work.

If Reg Park, a boy from a small English factory town, can become Mr. Universe and subsequently a movie star, why can't I?

If millions of European immigrants can come to America with nothing more than a suitcase and a dream, why can't I?

Why can't I become governor of California if Ronald Reagan, an actor, can?

And if I can do it, why can't you?

To be sure, I'm a madman. I don't act like a normal person. My dreams are not typical. My risk tolerance for ambitious goals and new difficulties is extreme. I go big with everything I do.

I worked out twice a day for four to five hours as a bodybuilder. As an actor, I took big risks in important films. In my first and only political post, I was in charge of the world's sixth-largest economy. My philanthropic concentration has been on environmental damage. My ambition is to contribute to the healing of the planet.

It's simply how I think. Big.

I often wonder what my life would be like if I didn't do things the way I do them. If only I could go back in time. If only my dreams had been smaller.

What if I had stayed in Austria and joined the police force like my father? What if I hadn't discovered bodybuilding, or if I'd maintained it as a hobby instead of making it a career? I've tried to envision what my life would have been like if I'd listened to the producers who advised me to alter my name, or if I'd let the opinions of reporters influence me when I told them I wanted to be an actor. What would it have looked like if "good enough" had sufficed?

I'm not sure. And I'm not interested in finding out. A life of half-baked dreams, doing some variation of what everyone else does? To me, that sounds like a gradual death. I'm not interested, and neither should you.

Why aim for the centre? Why settle for "good enough" before putting in the effort to see what you're capable of? What have you got to lose? It's not like having a huge vision requires more energy than having a modest one. Try it. Take out a piece of paper and a pencil. Make a mental note of your vision. Now cross that out and rewrite it larger. The same amount of energy, as you can see.

It is no more difficult to think big than it is to think tiny. The only difficult thing is giving yourself permission to think in that manner. Well, I don't just give you permission; I demand it, because when you're thinking about your objectives and creating your life vision, you have to understand that it's not just about you. You have the potential to have a significant impact on those around you. While you are breaking new ground in your own life, you may be blazing trails for individuals you are unaware are watching.

These things matter: how large your dreams are, whether you give it your all or give up at the first hint of difficulties. They are obviously important for your own pleasure and success. They also matter because they have the potential to make a significant influence in the world, well beyond what you can personally impact.

CHAPTER 3

WORK YOUR ASS OFF

I'm sure we have a lot in common. We are not the most powerful, intelligent, or wealthy people we know. We're not the quickest or most connected. We're not the most attractive or talented people. We lack superior genetics. But we do have something that many of those other folks do not: the desire to work. If there is one unchangeable truth in life, it is that there is no replacement for hard work. There is no shortcut, growth hack, or magic drug that will get you out of doing your job successfully, winning something important to you, or making your ambitions come true. For as long as hard labour has been difficult, people have attempted to cut corners and skip steps in the process. Those individuals eventually fall behind or are left in our dust, since working your tail off is the only thing that works 100% of the time for 100% of the things worth achieving. Consider something to which most of us can relate: being wealthy. It's fairly amazing when you consider that some of the happiest people you'll ever meet are lottery winners and people with inheritance money. According to some estimates, 70% of lottery winners go bankrupt within five years. Depression, suicide, and alcohol and drug misuse are all more common among the generationally wealthy than among the middle class or those who worked hard to achieve their fortunes.

There are several reasons for this, but one major one is that new-money lotto winners and old-money rich individuals never received any of the rewards that come from working toward a huge objective. They've never known what it's like to make money; they've just known what it's like to have it. They never had the opportunity to absorb the valuable lessons that struggle and failure produce. And they certainly did not receive the benefits of effectively applying those lessons to their dream.

Imagine Sir Edmund Hillary being helicopter to the peak of Mount Everest instead of walking there for two months in the spring of 1953. Do you believe the view from the top would have been as lovely? Do you think he cared about the other, smaller mountain he saw in the distance while he was up there? Certainly not! If you don't get to feel what it's like to push yourself, to do more than you thought you were capable of, and to know that the pain you put yourself through will lead to growth that you alone are responsible for creating, you'll never appreciate what you have the way someone who earned it, who worked for it does.

Work is effective. That is the end result. Regardless of what you do. Regardless of who you are. That single thought has impacted my entire existence.

For fifteen years, I trained five hours a day to become the greatest bodybuilder ever. When I moved to America, I upped my workouts and devised the double split, in which I trained for two and a half hours in the morning and two and a half hours in the evening, simply to get two full workouts in each day. Because no one wanted to train so hard, I required two sets of training partners: Franco in the morning and Ed Corney or Dave Draper in the evening. They weren't as insane as I was. At my peak, on my heaviest days, I was lifting 40,000 pounds every workout. That's the size of a fully loaded semi truck. The majority of people did not want to work that way. It was excruciatingly painful. But I enjoyed all of the reps. I desired all of the agony. So much so that my first Austrian trainer believed I was crazy. He was most likely correct.

When I quit from bodybuilding and moved into acting, I dedicated those five daily training hours to the process of becoming a leading man. I took acting classes, English and speech classes, and accent reduction classes (for which I still want my money back). I attended numerous meetings and read hundreds of screenplays, including those provided to me for consideration as well as any others I could get my hands on, in order to discover the difference between a bad script, a good script, and a fantastic script.

Then there was the work that went beyond simply reading the script and memorise my lines for each film. It was dance and improv instruction on Twins. It was becoming a machine on The Terminator: blindfolding myself until I could do every gun act with my eyes closed, and shooting so many rounds at the range that I no longer blinked when my gun discharged. On Terminator 2, it was practising the shotgun cocking flip until my knuckles bled—all for two seconds of screen time. I made no complaint. It was all part of the preparation for breaking the mould and becoming a new type of leading man—an action hero.

I then applied that theory to politics. During my 2003 campaign, I consumed briefing volumes on every issue that was relevant in California. Each one was chock-full of lengthy documents written by top experts on obscure topics I never dreamed I'd have to think about, let alone care about or maybe make choices on. Microstamping on gun ammunition and nurse-to-patient staffing ratios in county hospitals are two examples. After my morning workouts down the hill in Venice, I opened my home to anyone wanting to teach me about governing, policy, and the issues that were important to Californians. I was determined to live up to and fulfil the promise I made to voters throughout my campaign to be a different sort of politician. So I changed those five hours of training that I'd previously spent to bodybuilding and subsequently to the craft of acting into a type of immersion program for the language of politics and governance. Every day, I studied and practised like a foreign exchange student attempting to acquire the local language, checking my notes and speaking from memory until the words came smoothly.

In every period of my career, the goal of all this hard work—all the reps, all the pain, all the follow-through, all the long hours—was the same. It's the same for anything special you might want to do with your life, whether it's starting a business, getting married, being a farmer, becoming a watchmaker, travelling the world, earning a raise and a promotion, going to the Olympics, managing an assembly line, or starting a nonprofit organisation. The goal is to be well-prepared. It is to be prepared to perform when the limelight shines, when opportunity knocks, when the cameras roll, and when a crisis strikes. Don't get me wrong: there is value and significance in working hard for the sake of working hard, but the actual reason is so that when the time comes for your goal to come true and your vision to become a reality... you don't flinch or hesitate.

Reps, Reps, Reps

Working out has always meant repetitions for me since I started bodybuilding. Not just doing reps, but also keeping track of them. I'd write my complete exercise on the whiteboard at the local weight-lifting club in Graz, down to the amount of sets and reps, and I wouldn't allow myself to go until I'd checked them all off. Years later, when I was preparing for movies, I kept track of how many times I read the entire script by writing tally marks on the front cover, and I didn't stop reading until I'd memorised every scene. (The only time I forgot a line was when Danny DeVito pranked me on the set of Twins by replacing my lunchtime cigar with one laced with marijuana.) I used to do the same thing on the opening page of my speech drafts as governor, and I still do it now when I give commencement and keynote talks. I knew if I got to ten reps, I could give a solid speech, but twenty reps meant I could smash it out of the park. The words would sound more natural, as if I were speaking spontaneously and from the heart. The more I practised the speech, the more of myself I'd have in the room, and the more probable the audience would feel linked to me and the thoughts I was sharing with them.

The main point is that they must be good representatives. Not sluggish, distracted, arched-back, noodle-arm, nonsense reps. You must utilise good grammar. You must finish the entire exercise. You must exert full effort. Remember, if already, then already! It makes no difference whether we're talking about a dead lift, a press conference, or a speech run-through. Every time, you must give it your best. Believe me, I'm speaking from experience. It only takes one blunder, one poor action, or one wrong word to derail and put you back.

The whole goal of doing a lot of reps is to build a foundation that will make you stronger and more resistant to stupid, unlucky blunders, whatever that means for you. The idea is to raise your load capacity so that when it comes time to do the important work—the stuff that people see and remember—you don't have to worry about whether you can accomplish it. You simply do it. Everything comes apart if you don't take the time to do things correctly. If you only do half of your reps and don't pay attention to the subtleties, the foundation you're constructing will be unstable and unreliable.

That's why they say in weapons training, "slow is smooth, smooth is fast." It's why first responders, such as paramedics and firefighters, train compulsively and again until the foundations of their occupations become second nature to them. It's so that when the shit hits the fan and the unexpected occurs—which it always does—they don't have to think about the mundane, life-saving aspects of their job, and they can use that extra mental space to deal with situations they've never seen before without wasting precious seconds.

While the stakes are substantially lower in most other areas of life, that notion holds true in the majority of them. Consider jazz and the saxophonist John Coltrane. Coltrane is widely regarded as one of the finest improvising jazz performers of all time. He created his own distinct style, dubbed "sheets of sound," in which he could appear to be playing all the notes at once. Playing with other jazz greats like Thelonious Monk and Miles Davis throughout the late 1950s and early 1960s, it's impossible to predict what Coltrane's saxophone will sound like from night to night. During the day, however, you could rely on his unwavering work ethic.

Coltrane practised all the time. According to another saxophonist from his period, Coltrane practised "25 hours a day." He would play through the full 256-page Thesaurus of Scales and Melodic Patterns on a regular basis, which is the musical equivalent of watching Bruce Lee do "wax on, wax off" and "paint the fence" for eighteen hours. Coltrane is said to have practised a single note for ten hours straight to perfect the tone and volume. His wife frequently discovered him sleeping with the mouthpiece still in his mouth at home. In an interview, he stated that when he was very concentrated on an idea, he would practise on and off all day and entirely lose track of how many total hours he'd practised.

What he practised in secret and what he performed in public appeared to be two distinct art forms, but they were inextricably linked. It was all his fundamentals work that made the spontaneous music he played onstage appear magical. Practice was regimented and regimented, predictable and monotonous. His playing was loose, spontaneous, and great. It was as if he didn't have to think about the notes at all, which he didn't. He couldn't because he couldn't. There could be no delay if his improvisational style was to mix with the styles of the other players on stage. There were no more valuable seconds to contemplate. He had to know what to do, where to go, and what move to make in the moment, just like a paramedic at the scene of an accident or a firefighter in a collapsing building.

If you're a sports enthusiast, it's akin to watching the top footballers, basketball players, hockey players, and ski racers train their trade before performing on the largest platforms. Every week, there are hours and hours of tedious shooting drills. There are kilometres of skating, skiing, and running focused on footwork, direction change, balance, and body weight shifting. Every practice includes hundreds, if not thousands, of reps of dribbling and passing drills. The intensity of John Coltrane's playing wowed audiences all over the world. People would exclaim, "Trane's on fire!" Few of those individuals understood that his passion onstage was powered by endless repeats of the most lifeless, dull material imaginable, which he practised while no one was looking. The same can be said for Stephen Curry on the basketball floor, Lionel Messi on the soccer field, Alex Ovechkin on the ice, and Hermann Maier on the mountain. They may blow our minds when the lights come on because they did all the gritty, hard work when no one was looking. This is where we must arrive. This is what we must do. We have to accept the mundane. We must master the essentials. We must perform them correctly and frequently. This is the only way we can establish that strong foundation and all that muscle memory so that we can perform when it counts. It's the simple part.

Pain Is Temporary

I would not be where I am now without the success of Conan the Barbarian, which would not have been the economic success or cult phenomenon that it became without the director, John Milius, kicking my a$$ all around Spain, where we shot the film.

Conan's fundamental creation was difficult enough. Then there was the hour of weight training every day to be in top physical condition, as I was naked the entire time. Then, thirty to forty times before filming days, I rehearsed each of my long speeches with a dialect coach. I studied sword play as well as fight choreography. For the pit-fighting scenes, I trained in wrestling and boxing. I learnt to ride camels, horses, and elephants. I learnt to jump from enormous boulders, climb and hang from long ropes, and fall from great heights. I basically attended another vocational school for wannabe action heroes.

On top of that, Milius had me performing all sorts of heinous things. Take after take, I climbed over rocks until my forearms bled. I fled away from wild dogs who had caught me and dragged me into a thorn bush. I bit a real, dead vulture, which prompted me to clean my mouth with alcohol after each take. (PETA would have been all over that one.) I tore a gash on my back on one of the first days of filming, requiring forty stitches.

Milius' response: "Pain is temporary, but this film will be permanent."

And he was correct, which is why none of it troubled me. Pain was merely the cost of doing the effort required to create a superb sword-and-sorcery film, as they were known. And if I was willing to pay that price, I'd be one step closer to realising my goal. Sacrifices are required to accomplish great things that last.

That is the allure of suffering. Not only is it transient, so you won't have to live with it indefinitely, but it also shows you whether you've begun to devote too much of yourself in pursuit of your dreams. If becoming great or accomplishing something extraordinary hasn't hurt or cost you anything, or at the very least made you uncomfortable, then I'm sorry to be the one to tell you that you're not working hard enough. You are not sacrificing everything that could be sacrificed in order to become everything that you could become.

But pain isn't just a sign of sacrifice; it's also a sign of future progress. In the gym, if an exercise doesn't start to hurt, I know I haven't done enough to unlock the muscle's growth potential. Reps increase strength, but agony increases size. That's why I craved the agony. That's why I was always smiling in images and film recordings from the gym back in the 1970s. I wasn't a sadist. It wasn't fun squatting 600 pounds till I couldn't breathe and wanted to vomit. I was smiling because I was feeling the ache of the job, which indicated that progress was on the way. With each excruciating rep, I was one step closer to realising my bodybuilding aspirations. That made me delighted because winning titles and standing on the top step of the podium with the championship trophy was the goal of all my hard work.

This is not the first time I've realised this about pain. Not by any means. Muhammad Ali famously stated that he did not begin counting sit-ups until they hurt. "They're the only ones that count," he told me. "That's what makes you a champion." Bob Dylan once remarked that every beautiful thing is the result of anguish.

You are probably aware that this is correct. I'm sure you've heard some of the catchphrases that convey this concept. Step outside of your comfort zone. Accept the suck. Lean into the discomfort. Do something that scares you every day. These are just other ways of saying that if you want to grow or be great, it's not going to be simple. It will cause some discomfort. Or quite a bit.

Instructors don't really start testing candidates for Navy SEALs and Army Rangers until they're utterly fucking miserable. They exhaust you, shout in your face, limit your calories, and keep you outside or in the water until you're freezing and shaking. And it's at this point that they try to drown you or crush your brain with small assessments of fine motor skills and coordination. Even so, they aren't actually testing for competency. They are unconcerned about your ability to execute the work. They're trying to see if you'll give up when the suffering becomes unbearable. They have little desire to improve their skills or grow physically. The development of skills comes later. And they know that a motivated candidate will do the physical component on their own time. They're seeking for character development. Which is sometimes the most crucial thing in the pursuit of greatness and huge visions.

Nothing creates character like tenacity in the face of adversity. Nothing undermines character more than giving in to hardship and quitting. Having said that, enduring suffering for no purpose is foolish. Masochism at its finest. But we're not talking about that kind of pain here—the kind that has no meaning. We're talking about productive discomfort. The kind that promotes growth, that establishes a foundation and character, and that moves you closer to realising your vision.

Haruki Murakami, the great Japanese novelist, once said, "I can bear any pain as long as it has meaning." Pain simply needs to have meaning to you for it to be manageable, as I've discovered over the years.

I shattered my leg skiing in Sun Valley, Idaho, just before Christmas 2006. I broke my femur. The human body's thickest bone. It's difficult to shatter your femur. It stings. It also necessitates emergency surgery to place a plate and screws, which is painful. Two weeks later, I was to be sworn in for my second term as governor. This usually consists of a ceremony with the chief justice of the California Supreme Court, followed by a speech. To put it another way, a lot of standing.

My team and the event staff knew the hardship that all of that standing would cause, so they offered to cancel the official ceremony and hold the swearing-in ceremony in my house until I healed. I'm not interested. So I had two choices: take painkillers and hope I didn't slur like a crazy person throughout my speech, or ignore the medications and make the speech clearly, knowing that standing still at the stage would ache like hell.

I can handle twenty minutes of agony. I can handle a full day of suffering. Whatever I did, my leg was fractured. And I was going to be in pain regardless of where I was—at home on the sofa or onstage in Sacramento. Why wouldn't I pick the kind of agony that included realising my dream of guiding California to a brighter future? Sharing moments like this was a part of that ambition. It was standing in front of the people to demonstrate that I will always advocate for the people. Even if it meant breaking a commitment, I would keep it. Being able to accomplish it meant a lot to me. As John Milius put it, the anguish was just transitory. The power of that moment, as well as the sense of success I felt following the horrific election the year before, will live with me for the rest of my life.

Follow Up, Follow Through

California caught fire ten months later, around the end of October 2007. On a Friday night, I went to bed with tales of a couple of fires raging across the state. On Saturday, I learned that it had grown to about three dozen. The worst of them, in terms of the threat to life and property, were centred in San Diego County and would eventually require the evacuation of more than 500,000 people, including 200,000 San Diegans. Thousands of them would end up at the Del Mar racetrack and Qualcomm Stadium, home of the San Diego Chargers of the National Football League.

A firestorm in a densely populated area was a nightmare scenario for the state. We'd been war-gaming, scenario planning, and emergency drills for disasters like this since we witnessed the devastation caused by Hurricane Katrina two years before. Government services at all levels failed the poor people, and over 1500 people died as a result. I pledged that if we ever found ourselves in a similar scenario, we would have the necessary personnel and resources in place as soon as possible, we would know what was going on from the start, and we would be extremely attentive to the victims and individuals on the front lines. That was the entire point of our preparation and emergency drills.

When it comes to the work of someone in a position of power, this is where many people go wrong. They'll think my job is done since, as governor, I made sure we had a plan, that we rehearsed for disasters, and that everyone knew their responsibilities. A governor, like the boss of a corporation or the manager of a team, has many tasks. They can't do everything, they reason. They must eventually delegate and trust that the plan they've set in place will work and that the people they've engaged to carry it out will deliver.

Except that you can't simply expect other people to do what you think they'll do or what they say they'll do. Especially in the moment of truth, whether it's on the verge of success or calamity. (Making your ideal a reality frequently necessitates the same amount of effort as avoiding a nightmare scenario from unfolding.) Things happen. Signals get mixed up. People are sluggish. Some folks are simply foolish. If you have a job to complete, a goal to attain, or a commitment to safeguard something or someone, and it's vital to you that everything goes as planned, it's up to you to follow through all the way.

By Saturday afternoon, it was clear that the situation in San Diego was poised to devolve into a farce. I could see it in my head. There were too many moving elements scattered across too broad an area, and events were changing too quickly to keep up. As night fell, evacuees began to pour into Qualcomm Stadium, and we still didn't have cots or enough water, and I realised there had to be other things we were lacking. We'd have to go down there ourselves if we wanted to make sure everything got done.

On the way down, we heard from Qualcomm employees about what they still needed: more water, obviously, but also diapers, infant formula, toilet paper, and, strangely, canine poop bags. You don't realise it until you're deep into a situation like a disaster response, but the most important items to focus on after basic shelter are newborn and senior care, followed by sanitation. We quickly contacted the head of the California Grocers Association, who dispatched his troops to get all of the supplies we requested and meet us there.

There were still no cots when we arrived at the stadium. What happened to them? Who owned them? Why hadn't they arrived yet? My colleagues and I asked everyone we could think of who may know the answer, and we told them to call everyone they knew who might know the answer. After a series of phone calls, we discovered that the cots were kept in a storage facility that had been sold by the person with whom we had originally leased, and the new owner had changed the locks, unaware that one of his units was full of cots that were an essential piece of California's disaster response plan. And there was no key!

This stuff isn't made up. Those cots might still remain in that storage facility if we hadn't been there to ask questions, follow up, and ensure that everyone around us did their part in solving the problem. Thank goodness it was only the cost we were looking for. It could have been a lot scarier, like at the Del Mar racetrack.

Just as we were about to leave on Sunday night, I received information that 700 residents of a nearby nursing home had been transported to Del Mar. The fact that they were safe was a big relief, but something about the circumstance irritated me. Anyone who has seen the medication cabinet of an elderly person with even a moderate number of medical concerns understands how hard their treatment is. It's not as simple as putting them in a bed inside an auditorium on the infield of a horse track in an emergency. So I stopped by Del Mar with my squad to check in.

The fact that there were no doctors on-site was the first cause for alarm. There was just one nurse, a Navy medic called Paul Russo, who was a total badass. He was in charge of all the care for these displaced men and women. The second sign appeared while I was strolling around as everyone was getting ready for bed, when a wonderful lady approached me, afraid and a little bewildered, and said, "I don't know what to do, tomorrow morning I'm supposed to go for my dialysis treatment."

This sparked a flood of follow-up queries. How many other people require immediate daily care, such as dialysis? How many of them would benefit from being in a hospital under the care of a doctor? Where is the nearest hospital with available space? What number of dialysis machines do they have? Do we have enough ambulances to transport everyone?

The rest of the night was spent figuring out the answers to those questions. We discovered that a few dozen people required medical attention, but there were no hospital beds within 150 miles to accommodate them. So we began contacting the leaders of each branch of the military, all of which had bases in California. As governor, you quickly realise that every base has two things: firearms and medical facilities. We discovered an empty wing at the hospital at Camp Pendleton, the nearby Marine post. We had beds; now we needed ambulances to transport all of these folks, which we located sixty miles north in Orange County. We worked from our jet all night, sleeping a few hours here and there while we sat on the tarmac, waiting for confirmation that everyone at Del Mar who needed to be evacuated had been relocated. It was arduous labour in harsh conditions, which is to be anticipated in a crisis, and we only took off and headed home after it was finished.

This is how you proceed. This is how you carry it out. It's all about not leaving any stone untouched. It's all about crossing your t's and dotting your i's. It's all about closing the circle and returning. I shudder to imagine what would have happened to some of those nursing home residents if we had done even 1% less than we did. And yet, so many people are willing to rely totally on plans and procedures, or to perform the bare minimum required, and then say to themselves, "This is all set, I took care of it." No. Don't be a slacker. Perform the necessary tasks. The only time you can say "I took care of it" is after it is completed. Completely.

I am obsessed with following through. In many ways, I consider following through to be the crux of the hard work required for significant things to get done, because important things are never simple or uncomplicated. It virtually always depends on timing, other people, and a number of moving parts—all of which are unpredictable. Ironically, follow-through is usually the simplest component of the job, at least in terms of energy and resources; yet it's virtually always the item we take for granted or let slide through the cracks. We declare, "I want to do this great, fantastic thing," and then we start the ball rolling, expecting it to keep rolling because we want it to. As if hope and good intentions aren't valuable.

This is something we even do to ourselves. It happens all the time in sports. When a golfer fails to follow through with their sand wedge in a greenside bunker, the ball either goes nowhere or soars across the green. During a point, a tennis player does everything correctly, positioning themselves to smash a backhand down the line, but they fail to follow through on their swing, and the ball flies out of the stadium. The same phenomenon happens when footballers fail to convert one-touch volleys into the box or even something as simple as a penalty kick. It happens in the gym as well. I can't tell you how many times I see guys on the lat pulldown machine who don't get the entire stretch at the top or the full flex at the bottom of the exercise. They don't literally follow up or follow through.

It may appear to be a little detail, but a lack of follow-through at any time can cause you to lose a match or potential winnings, just as it can cause you to lose out in life. It's a sign that you're not entirely committed, that you're not going all in, that you're just going through the motions. This is a much greater issue than you realise, since if you accept a poorly executed shot attempt or a half-assed lat workout from yourself as acceptable, you're more inclined to accept half-assed versions of other, more significant things from yourself. Things like your work production. Or how you present yourself in your relationship. Or even how you care for your child. The person who is content with four sets of ten shitty half reps on the pulldown machine is more likely to sloppily change their baby's diaper or forget their partner's order at their favourite restaurant than the person who struggles through five sets of fifteen painful but perfect reps, even if it takes longer and exhausts them. I'd say especially then, because such folks know what it's like to work hard and accomplish things well.

According to Woody Allen, showing up is responsible for 80% of one's achievement in life. Before him, Thomas Edison stated that perspiration accounts for 90% of accomplishment. They are not incorrect, but they cannot both be correct. The maths is flawed. Jimmy Dean, an American country musician and sausage maker, I believe, nailed it. He concluded by saying, "Do what you say you're going to do, and try to do it a little better than you said you would."

Completely follow up and follow through. Do just those two things, which I know you can if your vision is important enough to you, and you will stand out from the crowd. Unlike the vast majority of people who claim to be motivated to achieve something meaningful or to make a difference, it will demonstrate that you are serious about putting in the effort to make your vision a reality.

There Are Twenty-Four Hours. Use Them.

I have some more excellent news to share with you. Aside from our willingness to labour, we share something else. We all have the same twenty-four hours in the day to do our tasks. Everything else in our life is different—age, money, where we live, what we're excellent at—but we both have the same drive and the same amount of time. That's wonderful! It signifies that if we put in the time and effort, there is nothing we can't achieve.

What you need to ask yourself is, "How much of that time am I wasting?" How much of it do I waste planning how I'm going to get started... instead of getting started? How much of it do I flush down the social media toilet? How much of my time do I spend watching TV, playing video games, drinking, and partying?

My wish for you is that you don't waste too much of your time. Unfortunately, many people squander their time. The biggest offenders are those who have huge, ambitious dreams and passionately want to alter their lives, but when I ask what they're doing to make those dreams a reality, they spend twenty minutes telling how busy they are. People who grumble the most about not having enough time, predictably, accomplish the least amount of work.

To put it another way, activity is nonsense. We've all been "busy." Every day, we all have responsibilities. Obligations and liabilities. We all need to eat, sleep, and pay our expenses. What does this have to do with putting in the effort to achieve your goals? Make the time if it is important to you.

By the mid-1970s, I'd accomplished a number of lofty objectives for myself. I'd arrived in America, having won the Mr. Universe and Mr. Olympia competitions. I was widely regarded as the greatest bodybuilder in the world. But the job wasn't done. Once you've achieved the peak, you must figure out how to stay there. For me, that meant partly moving my sights to Hollywood, which held the promise of even greater success, but first I had to spend some time in Los Angeles carving up a comfortable life for myself while still doing the work required to be in competition shape.

First, I prepared bodybuilding booklets and negotiated a deal with Joe Weider that if he gave me a double-page spread in the middle of his magazines to sell my booklets, he wouldn't have to pay me for the photo sessions I performed for his supplements or equipment. Then I began attending classes at Santa Monica City College and UCLA, largely in business. To supplement my income, I gave weight-lifting workshops, and Franco and I started a masonry firm, doing bricklaying work all around town. I acquired an apartment complex and became a landlord using the money I earned from bricklaying and booklet sales. And when I eventually decided to make a more definite move toward Hollywood, that's when I started taking all those acting and improv lessons I mentioned before. My dancing calendar was completely booked... with dance classes!

Of course, I didn't do any of these things at random. Aside from the fact that they either made or might one day save me money, I was always thinking about my ambitions. I did the bodybuilding publications so that I could reach more people and the sport could reach more people. It was also a means for folks who couldn't afford to attend one of my seminars to get support.

I selected bricklaying since it was like an extra workout for me. I got to work on my tan and practise my English on strangers, and I got to experience the sense of accomplishment that comes from making things. Remember, my goal was not simply to come to America; it was to become a part of America. Being in movies helped, but there are still walls and walkways in Los Angeles that Franco and I built together between workouts fifty years ago that I consider to be part of my legacy, alongside my star on the Hollywood Walk of Fame and billboards with my face on Sunset Boulevard.

I took business lessons in order to study and perhaps become fluent in the language of American business. I also wanted to prepare for the business side of show business so that I didn't get taken advantage of by agencies or studios.

I acquired an apartment complex so I could have a place to live and not have to worry about rent, which has traditionally been one of the big motivations driving ambitious performers to take lousy jobs that weren't part of their professional ambition. I had no desire to be a working actor. I aspired to be a starring man and an action hero. Because I had a roof over my head, I could be patient and turn down offers for minor roles like a Nazi soldier or a skinhead bouncer.

People are surprised when I tell them about my days back then, even when I explain why they were so full, as I just did to you.

"When did you have time to eat?" they will inquire. I'll tell them that most of the time I ate like any other person. If I was short on time, I'd eat in the car on the way to the gym or while studying. Every morning in class, I'd have my protein shake. And on the rare instances when I didn't have time to eat... Well, I just didn't. A missed supper has never killed anyone.

Others will ask, "When did you ever have fun?" I'll say I was always having a good time. Why would I bust my a$$ like that if it wasn't entertaining? I like training. Franco taught me how to lay bricks, which I thoroughly enjoyed. I enjoyed meeting new people and learning about American business practices.

"When did you sleep?" is an often asked question. I'd slumber after my morning workout or in the truck while the mortar dried on a wall we were constructing. But when I felt exhausted, I'd typically just sleep.

"Weren't you always tired?" That is the inevitable follow-up inquiry. And my answer is always the same: no. To be honest, I've always had a lot of energy, dating back to when I was a youngster, so some of this is inherited. But the greater, more significant component is the one that so many people overlook. There's nothing more exciting than making progress when you're chasing a vision and working toward a major objective.

When an idea from one of my business classes sparked for me during my studies, I knew I had to delve deeper. When I heard my English improving, I wanted to talk to more people and practise more. When I felt the pump at the gym, I knew I was making progress, and it made me want to lift until my arms fell off. Sometimes I did. I'd lift till I felt the pump, then keep going until I truly felt the agony, like Ali mentioned, and then keep going until I couldn't move anymore. There were days when this was the only way you could get me out of the gym. And, while I was physically fatigued, I was mentally sharp as a tack. I was ecstatic and energised because I'd just spent two hours getting closer to my goal.

How could you expect me to sleep in such a situation?

This is the state of mind that people refer to when they talk about entering a "flow state." Time extends and contracts at the same time.

You get into something, start making progress, and then all of a sudden, you look up and it's morning.

Writers, singers, computer programmers, chess masters, architects, artists, and anyone with a true enthusiasm for a hobby all have stories like these. Stories of people doing work that appears to defy the constraints of human attention span and physiology, when time should have caught up with them and shut down their minds. And that does happen from time to time, like when John Coltrane falls asleep with his saxophone still in his lips, or a video-game designer passes out on their keyboard, or a detective falls asleep surrounded by case files. But almost as frequently, you'll find software developers participating in 36-hour hackathons to create games or apps that will alter the world. Or you get a narrative like Sam Peckinpah reworking The Wild Bunch script over three days in the desert. Or you might have Black Sabbath record their debut album in a single twelve-hour session. Or, after a long day in the studio, Keith Richards comes up with the riff for "Satisfaction" as he's ready to fall asleep.

Whether it's a matter of getting into flow state or not, everyone who gets stuff done has one thing in common: they either find the time, make the time, or turn the time they do have into what it takes to complete the task at hand. If you're still concerned about eating, energy, sleep, or enjoyment after hearing these stories, it's possible that your issue isn't one of time at all. Perhaps it's how you spend your time. Do you know how many times people say they don't have time to exercise, and then I ask them to take out their phones and show me their screen time numbers, which indicate they spent three and a half hours on social media? It's not a lack of hours in the day that you're looking for; it's a vision for your life that makes time meaningless.

Perhaps you have an outstanding, compelling goal that motivates you, but the time required to realise it is so long that the road to achievement has become daunting and paralysing. That is a real possibility, and it can be very frightening. I understand. Building a body to compete in bodybuilding contests did not happen immediately, over a year, or even over two or three years. It required several years of consistent, everyday labour that no one paid me to perform to bring my physique to the size and proportion that drew the notice of judges, Joe Weider, and the general public. It required even more years to fine-tune my figure and keep it in shape to win successive Mr. Olympia championships and play parts like Conan and the Terminator.

I would have suffocated if I had concentrated solely on the ultimate product or attempted to consume the elephant in one bite, as the adage goes. I would have been a failure. The only way to achieve the kind of long-term, life-changing achievement I want was to put in the hard, incremental effort day after day. I have to concentrate on getting the reps in and executing correctly. I needed to listen to the suffering and build on the eventual growth. Every day, I had to carry out the plan I devised in pursuit of my broader vision.

The same ideas apply to you, no matter what you're attempting to do or how hectic your life is right now. I'll show you how here. Let's try something I call The 24-Hour Countdown:

How many hours do you sleep per day? Let's pretend it's eight hours, because that's what current research shows is optimal for peak performance and longevity. There are now sixteen hours left in the day.

How many hours a day do you work? Let's pretend that's also eight hours. We now have eight hours left in the day.

How long does your everyday commute take? The typical daily commute in the United States is slightly under a half hour each way, but to account for folks who live near major cities, let's round it to forty-five minutes each way. That takes around an hour and a half. We're now down to six and a half hours.

How much time do you spend with your family during the day, including breakfast, supper, and watching TV? Let's say three and a half hours, which is fantastic. That is true quality time. We now have three hours left in the day.

How much time do you spend each day working out or being physically active? Most people spend around an hour on average, including time spent walking the dog, doing housework, and working out. Fantastic, an hour of activity per day is essential. We've got two hours left.

After accounting for everything in a regular day, there are still two hours in the day to work toward your objective. I can already hear a few of you asking, "What about time for rest and relaxation?" To begin with, rest is for babies, and relaxation is for the elderly. Which of these are you? If you want to do something extraordinary, if you have a huge ambition that you want to realise, I believe you'll have to put relaxing on the back burner for a while. But if you want to unwind, take half of the remaining time for a short nap. That still leaves you with one hour per day to work on your objective.

Do you realise how powerful an hour a day may be? If you want to write a novel, set aside an hour every day and strive for one page. You will have a 365-page manuscript by the end of the year. That's the title of a book! If you want to lose weight, you should burn 500 more calories each day than you consume. That's a pound you'll have lost in a week. That may be fifty pounds in a year! How can you burn more calories than you consume? Use that extra hour to go on a bike ride. Even if you ride at a reasonable pace five days a week, you will have ridden more than the distance between Los Angeles and Boston at the end of a year. You'll have travelled across the country!

These are wonderful achievements that necessitate a lot of hard work. But it's work you can do if you prepare ahead of time and break it down into little, daily goals that shouldn't take more than an hour or two to achieve. Even if you're insane like me, it's only five hours of labour per day. That leaves you with nineteen hours to complete the rest of your tasks. Eat a little faster, take fewer breaks on your commute, and sleep a little faster, and you'll have discovered the hours you require. So don't tell me you don't have time to train, study, write, network, or do whatever else is required to attain your vision.

Turn off the television. Throw your equipment out the window. Save your excuses for someone who is interested. Start working.

CHAPTER 4

SELL, SELL, SELL

One of the biggest culture shocks I faced when I first moved to America was the lack of cultural awareness regarding bodybuilding. I was anticipating a lot more from the sport after reading about it in Joe Weider's magazines. Don't get me wrong: the bodybuilding subculture was clearly present. We had magazines and nutritional supplements with us. We had our own tournament circuit, complete with titles and awards. There were fantastic bodybuilding gyms all around the country, including two major ones in Los Angeles, where I was living. There were also fans and groupies. However, few people outside of the bodybuilding world were familiar with the sport. When I met someone at a party or talked with a stranger in line at the store and they noticed how built I was (which wasn't difficult because I strolled around in shorts and tank tops all the time), they'd say things like, "Wow, look at those muscles, what are you, a football player?" "No, guess again," I'd answer, and they'd say something like a wrestler or a bouncer. They would never suspect I was a bodybuilder.

I saw that major media and sports publications were not covering bodybuilding. We were also ignored by television networks. And when they did, they covered a competition in the same way that they do today's Nathan's Famous International Hot Dog Eating Contest. We were an attraction. It's my first. You could tell by the way they described us. The phrases "muscle-bound" and "freak" (or "freakish") occurred in practically every account. They were continually implying that we were ignorant, queer, or selfish. This perplexed me. Why did being in top physical condition seem strange to them? And why were those the only options available?

Why were they so preoccupied with our posing shorts or the oil we'd apply to accentuate muscle definition? They'd disregard the years of hard work and sacrifice we'd all made, then reduce a world championship competition to the most basic visual: a group of tanned, shiny men flexing next to one another onstage, clearly overcompensating for what must be lacking inside the very little clothing we were wearing.

I questioned some of the American guys at Gold's why things were the way they were. They had no idea. "We should talk to these journalists!" But, as I mentioned, the majority of the guys were against it. They said that all of those writers and reporters were biassed or jealous, which is why they were always so unkind to us. "Why would this time be any different?" they wondered. That, however, did not make sense to me. How would a writer know how many hours we work per day? How would they know how much weight we have to lift, how strong we are, or how disciplined we must be? If we didn't inform them, how would they know any of this? My bodybuilding friends refused to speak with the media because they consistently misrepresented who we were and what we did, but refusing to speak with them was how we got ourselves into this situation of misunderstanding in the first place.

I was one of the gym's youngest members at the time, but I'd had enough experience doing sales-type jobs in Europe to know that if you want to acquire awareness for anything and build your business, even if it's an odd sport, you have to tell people about it. You must communicate and market it so that people are aware of its existence. So they understand what's going on and why they should care. To put it another way, you must sell it.

That's our responsibility, I told the lads, to explain to the general public what bodybuilding is.

Newspapers, television shows, and journalists? They should not be our adversaries, but rather our allies. They require stories to fill their pages and air time just as much as we require stories to be told. If we want the sport to grow, we should fill those buckets of space with our own descriptions of our sport and ideas about what makes it unique. We couldn't expect them to fill those buckets as well as we could, and we couldn't bank on them to fill that area as well. Consider what occurred when they were left to their own devices. If we wanted to improve the image of bodybuilding, we had to educate the media, and hence the general public. We had to be the ones to explain the sport, promote it, and sell it to them. When entrepreneurs, athletes, and artists ask me for guidance these days—whether it's about their newest product, their latest work, or how to acquire representation—the one thing I tell them is that they should do more advertising. Communicating. Selling. Selling, selling, selling! You can have the most incredible concept, the most brilliant strategy, the best in class of almost anything, but if no one knows it exists or what it is, it's a waste of time and effort. It could just as well not exist at all. You cannot allow it to happen when it comes to attaining your dreams. In fact, it should never happen since no one is better suited or driven to sell your idea to the rest of the world than you. It makes no difference whether you want to relocate your family to another nation or your football team to a new town, whether you want to produce movies or make a difference, whether you want to start a business, purchase a farm, join the military, or develop an empire. Whatever the enormity of your dream, you must know how to sell it and to whom you must sell it.

Know Your Customer

Selling your vision is being upfront about your goals and expressing your story in such a way that it is regarded positively by the individuals you need or want to receive a yes from. In other words, your customers.

When I first started acting and subsequently transitioned from action pictures to comedy, I had to sell my vision to agents, directors, producers, and studio executives so they would say yes and give me a chance in their films. The entire dog-and-pony show Ivan, Danny, and I put on in Tom Pollock's office to get Twins created was essentially a sales routine for one huge customer trying to decrease his risk. Our task was to give Tom a story that made our film's vision appear to be exactly what he was looking for.

"Listen," I continued, "believe me, we're all on the same page." For this film, we share the same artistic vision. There are no egos in this place."

"I know exactly how I'm going to shoot this, Tom," Ivan remarked. "Just give us the sixteen million, and I'll bring this thing in on time and on budget."

"Then we can all share in its success," Danny explained. "And you won't have to worry about salaries at all."

Tom extended his hand across the desk and shook ours. He recognized that this was a fantastic bargain for everyone, and he was ready to demonstrate just how fantastic he thought it was for us. He sat back in his chair, emerged from behind his desk, knelt, and flipped his pants pockets inside out.

"Do you know what you just did to me?" he blurted out. "You just robbed and fucked me blind." That's exactly what you did. Congratulations."

We were all laughing. Another happy customer!

As I began to land starring roles, I realised that I needed to market myself and my films to people other than producers and executives. I had to prove to moviegoers that I was a fine actor, and I had to persuade critics that my films were works of art. And by good, I don't simply mean good in terms of quality; I also mean good for society.

The first time this happened on a large scale was when The Terminator was released. Many journalists were only interested in discussing the film's brutality. They questioned why I wanted to play a killing machine in my next role after all the fictitious murdering I did in the Conan films. It may seem quaint now, but recall that in the early 1980s, movie critics were extremely important. Critics such as Gene Siskel, Roger Ebert, Pauline Kael, Rex Reed, and Leonard Maltin can kill your film with a negative review.

I made a conscious choice that anytime I was asked about violence in interviews leading up to the premiere of The Terminator, I would respond directly to the critiques. I asked one reporter if they'd read the Bible, knowing that it's one of the bloodiest texts ever written by body count. I informed another reporter that the film was science fiction, that my character was a machine, and that technology was a warning to humanity. I stated that Jim Cameron's script was, by definition, 100 percent pro-human. I told the version of The Terminator narrative that was genuinely Jim's purpose at every opportunity, not the one that all these random journalists seemed keen to write. The ultimate product speaks for itself: the film was a box-office hit and received positive reviews from critics across the board.

I was lucky in that it was rather evident to whom I needed to sell. It might be just as evident for you if you take the time to study your own environment. The people you need to sell will approach you, and you may direct your attention to them.

Assume you wish to pursue your passion for pottery throwing. You have a goal of creating gorgeous dishes and selling them at a local farmers market or on your own website. This dream does not require the approval of anyone. There are no barriers to entering the world of pottery... unless you want to take out a loan to purchase all of the necessary equipment and supplies. Then you need a bank (or a relative or a friend with money) to say yes, which means they are now your customer, and it is your responsibility to sell them on this vision.

But suppose you don't need a loan; there's still the issue of the folks you want to hear yes from just to make sure they're on your side. In this situation, it could be your partner or your parents, who are concerned that if you drop out of school or your job, you would run out of money and go bankrupt. They aren't sceptics in the usual sense; they are simply afraid—of you and of themselves. Your objective is to persuade them of your vision in order to reassure them and move them from a probable no to a yes, or at the very least an OK. Obviously, you do not need their permission to pursue your desire, and you should not be discouraged if it does not come, but if you can persuade them, it is always preferable to have more people on your side.

I learned a lot about selling as a youngster in Austria, both at vocational school and as an apprentice at a hardware store in Graz. I did everything you'd expect a hardware shop employee to do: deliveries, inventory and restocking, sweeping, bookkeeping, customer service, and, of course, sales. It was on the floor, observing the owner, Herr Matscher, that I learnt the most about selling and why people buy what they do—not just items and services, but also ideas.

Herr Matscher could sell anything to anyone because he paid attention to and tuned into them. I recall a couple and woman coming in one afternoon to look at tiling. Herr Matscher cordially greeted the wife before turning his attention to the husband, as was typical in a culture such as Austria's in the early 1960s, because he was the head of the household. Herr Matscher took out a number of tiles and placed them in front of the pair. He began describing the advantages and disadvantages of each hue and style to his husband. He inquired as to whether the man preferred one style over another, or one hue over another. He inquired as to what room the tile would be installed in, his budget, and when they would require the tile. The husband rapidly became irritated by all of my questions, which perplexed me. Herr Matscher's queries were all routine and required. A typical consumer would be irritated if these questions were not asked. Then I noticed Her Mother's body shifting toward his wife. She was intrigued by his inquiries. She had strong feelings about the tiles. She was conversing with him and taking in what he said.

Herr Matscher realised he had been speaking to the wrong person. The husband may have made the money, but it was the wife's perspective and decision that was important. She knew exactly what they were going to do with the tile. Her spouse couldn't care less; he was only there to make her happy and to write the money. Technically, he was the buyer, but she was the true customer. Herr Matscher needed to gain approval from her. He immediately focused all of his attention on the woman, and after an extended conversation that excluded the husband entirely, they reached a conclusion.

"What do you think, my dear?" she asked her spouse.

"Yes, yes, whatever you want," he murmured, not glancing at the tile she'd chosen.

Herr Matscher gave him the whole cost invoice, and he wrote a check on the spot without question.

"What did you just learn?" Herr Matscher told me after the couple had left.

"How to sell our merchandise," I asked, not knowing what he was actually asking.

"Yes, but that's just one thing," he explained. "Did you notice how I switched gears and began paying attention to the woman?" I did this because she was in charge of the purchase. She suggested that they have tiles for their bathroom. It was her idea what colour they should be. So I concentrated on her."

"I noticed that," I mentioned.

"When a couple or a group comes in," he explained, "you need to figure out who is in charge, who is passionate about whatever you're selling, and who engages the most with you." You must understand who the client is, who the boss is, and who makes the decisions."

That interaction and what it taught me about paying attention and tuning into others will be with me forever. You should never assume that you know who your customer is. It's not always clear who needs to be moved toward a yes and who needs to be moved away from a no. It's impossible to know for certain who your vision is attracting positively or adversely until you pay attention to who is paying attention to you.

Seeing how the world around you reacts to what you're attempting to do is an important component of selling your idea. It is how you determine who wants to say yes and who needs to say yes. If you can accomplish this, you will know who all of your consumers are before they even realise you are selling to them.

Make Mountains out of MOLEHILLS

When you think about it, you are your first customer. The goal of crystallising your vision and planning out how it will be realised is to sell yourself on the potential of your own desire. But soon, you'll have to sell it to the rest of the globe as well. Speaking your inner voice out loud so others can hear it is one of the simplest and most honest ways to begin selling it. Everything you tell yourself about what you're going to accomplish, you should start telling other people.

Some people need to publicly commit to their goal because they get caught up in planning rather than execution. It is always easier to dream than to act. Making a public commitment to a large goal is an excellent approach to get started. It is also an important step for many of us who require others to know about our dreams in order for them to come true. This may include launching a restaurant, an auto shop, or a political campaign—anything that requires customers or supporters in some way. If you want people to know about your hobby, you must inform them. And if you truly want to increase the exposure of your idea to the world, don't simply tell people about it; behave as if it's already come true. You accomplish this by freely discussing your goals while eliminating the phrase "will be" from your language.

It is not "I will become a great bodybuilder." said "I can see myself as a great bodybuilder."

It isn't, "I will be a leading man." Then again, "I can picture myself as a leading man."

This is common practice at political campaign rallies. It doesn't say, "Please welcome to the stage, the man who will be the next governor of California . . ." It has to be "Please welcome to the stage, the next governor of California . . ."

Saying things in this manner is really effective for two reasons: First, it shows your vision to the world as if it were genuine, forcing you to work hard right now to make it a reality. Second, in circumstances when you require other people to believe in your idea for it to succeed, making it sound as if it has already achieved success is the ultimate marketing. Giving individuals the impression that their dream has come true is a cry to arms for those who want to be a part of your company, movement, or whatever it is.

Joe Weider and his brother, Ben, were geniuses. They didn't say things like, "Bodybuilding will be a huge sport one day." "Bodybuilding is a huge sport," they claimed, and they disseminated that idea everywhere they could. On promotional tours to foreign countries, they would convince local leaders, "Bodybuilding is nation-building." They were attempting to establish a network of worldwide bodybuilding federations. What a phrase!

As a young boy in the early 1960s, reading their magazines and seeing their commercials, I had no reason to doubt that bodybuilding was everything the Weiders claimed it to be. It has to be a popular sport with fans all over the world. After all, bodybuilding champions have appeared in films. They appeared on magazine covers and in photographs with attractive women in well-known locations such as Muscle Beach. They were promoting products. That's not going to happen unless bodybuilding is big, right?

Wrong.

When I arrived at Venice Beach in late 1968, I quickly discovered that Joe had exaggerated things slightly. Muscle Beach had been closed for almost a decade. Bodybuilders weren't seen wandering around with surfboards in one hand and a blond female in a bikini in the other. They were neither wealthy nor famous. Weider Nutrition, which I assumed was a big operation at the centre of the bodybuilding industry, but at the heart of industry in general, was actually simply a typical successful American corporation. They had a large number of personnel spread across various offices selling a large lot of stuff, but the planes with the Weider name on them that I had seen in his magazines didn't exist. He had chartered a jet for a picture shoot and defaced it with a bogus insignia. That didn't matter to me, though. Joe had persuaded me and millions of others like me over the years that America was the place for us to realise our dreams and take the next step on our paths to prosperity. Los Angeles was also where I needed to go in order to take the next step. Furthermore, as a dedicated twenty-one-year-old full of energy, the fact that I had to put in a bit more effort than I anticipated in order to make bodybuilding mainstream was no sweat on my back. Joe had filled the bucket sufficiently to propel the sport to the point where it drew me in and brought me to America. It was now my turn to fill the bucket, sell the concept, expand the sport even further, and attract everyone else. I hired a publicist, who assisted me in landing appearances on The Dating Game, The Mike Douglas Show, and, subsequently, The Tonight Show with Johnny Carson. To supplement my training books, I held bodybuilding seminars across the country to raise awareness and educate people who were interested. I made myself available for any opportunity to tell the story of bodybuilding the way Joe and I both believed it should be told, which included speaking with Charles Gaines and George Butler in 1973 for their book, Pumping Iron, which laid the groundwork for the rest of the decade.

In the summer of 1974, I conducted an interview with a journalist for the Los Angeles Times in which I was able to dispel all of the myths about bodybuilding and explain what the sport was all about. I sold the sport to the reporter in the same way that Joe had sold it to me through his articles. The result was a lengthy, fair piece that dubbed me "the Babe Ruth of bodybuilding" and included a full-length photo that ran on the top page of the sports section with a headline boasting about how much money I could make only from bodybuilding. A few months later, Sports Illustrated published a piece about the Mr. Olympia event, which was held at Madison Square Garden that year, and it used the same terminology that a sportswriter would use to describe the greatest athletes in the most popular mainstream sports of the day.

Mr. Olympia would be shown on American television for the first time only two years later, on ABC's Wide World of Sports. Famous artists such as Andy Warhol, Robert Mapplethorpe, Leroy Neiman, and Jamie Wyeth would photograph and paint me. In February 1976, Frank Zane, Ed Corney, and I were asked to pose for a group of art historians and critics at the Whitney Museum in New York for an exhibit called "Articulate Muscle: The Male Body in Art," which Sports Illustrated described as an opportunity to look at us "not in athletic terms, but as artists living inside our own creations." The event was so well-attended that the museum ran out of seats and had to ask the majority of attendees to sit on the floor!

At the start of the decade, it seemed impossible to imagine that the "muscle-bound freaks" of this strange little subculture would be called artists or works of art, or that publications like the Los

Angeles Times and Sports Illustrated would run legitimate news stories about us. Nonetheless, here we were. We'd made it. By properly positioning myself as the face of bodybuilding, I was able to assist us in eventually presenting and explaining the sport in a way that pushed the narrative toward what we were all attempting to achieve.

Bodybuilding had progressed from a subculture to a part of culture by 1975 or 1976. By the end of the decade, everyone from dancers to doctors had tried weight lifting. People were lifting to look well, feel good, and improve their overall fitness. Weights were being used as part of physical therapy and rehabilitation. Athletes in other sports were also lifting more to get a competitive advantage. As a result, gyms began to spring up all over the place. Joe, I believe, was anticipating all of this. It's also why he paid for my ticket and set me up in the beginning. He knew I was the type of hustler who would sell the shit out of bodybuilding in order to make my own dream come real, which would also make his dream come true. This is the fundamental differentiator in Joe Weider's work that, if recognized, can unleash the full power of your vision. Joe used salesmanship to make bodybuilding appear to be more than it was, but every decision he made and move he took after that was focused at making those marketing promises a reality. As a dreamer, marketer, and self-promoter, he projected to the world where he believed bodybuilding and his own business could go if he kept doing what he was doing. He was showing anyone who had a similar desire the road map and the destination, and if you wanted to join him on his quest to make bodybuilding mainstream, you could play a significant role in making it happen. It wasn't a lie that he hadn't arrived yet. It was a question of when, not if. Every year, the fitness industry generates $100 billion in income.

Joe was a forerunner. Many of today's most famous entrepreneurs have unknowingly followed in his footsteps, because his style of advertising and selling is how successful Silicon Valley start-ups, such as Airbnb, set a road to becoming global billion-dollar "unicorns." Instead of talking about the revolutionary potential for the average person to spend the night in someone's home anywhere in the world, the company's founders should have talked about their original idea of being a hospitality alternative for people attending conferences in cities where all the hotel rooms were booked up. Even if the founders had stated, "Hey, we're ready to grow beyond this idea and are excited to see where it could lead!" Nobody was going to bite unless they also articulated and sold the wider goal as if they were already halfway down that specific business path. This much I learned early on from Joe. I like this inspiring saying: "See it. Consider it. Get it done." But I believe it is lacking a step in the middle: Please explain. I believe you must declare your goals before you can accomplish them. Distribute them. I believe you must admit to yourself, and explain to others, that what began in your head as a small concept has grown into a massive dream with enormous potential to enrich your life and theirs.

Let Them Underestimate You

A skilled salesman understands that giving the customer more than they expected and leaving them feeling like they're always getting the better end of the bargain is the key to making a sale and creating a customer for life. When you're selling yourself, the easiest approach to consistently surpass expectations is to keep them as low as possible. Or, perhaps a better way to say it, you shouldn't be afraid to let your consumer have their low expectations since it will make it that much simpler for you to blow them away and sell them on what you have to offer.

I participated in a televised debate with the four other prominent contenders two weeks before the recall election in 2003. This was the pivotal moment in that insane campaign. Five hundred journalists filed for credentials to attend. At least sixty cameras were present in the room. The discussion was live-streamed on all national cable news networks as well as every local network station in the state. According to that week's survey, two-thirds of potential voters felt the outcome of the debate will have a substantial impact on who they voted for. Lieutenant Governor Cruz Bustamante, the main Democratic contender, was leading going into the election. Nobody knew what to expect, but based on the news coverage leading up to the discussion, everyone expected me to fall flat on my face.

For weeks, all I could think about was my credibility. Is he a professional actor? Is he a bodybuilder? Does he have any suggestions? Is he really so smart? Does he really care because he's wealthy and famous? How is he qualified to manage forty million people and the world's sixth-largest economy?

I won't lie: all of these inquiries were incredibly annoying to my ego. I'd been dealing with this kind of doubt since I first arrived in America, at every level and in every venue, for what I assume is the same reason each time: no one had ever seen somebody like me before. There weren't many guys going around Los Angeles carrying 235 pounds of muscle in the 1970s. In the 1980s, Hollywood lacked action heroes who appeared to be capable of killing bad guys. There were no leading males with muscles that were as thick as their accent. When I went on my first late-night talk show, I answered the most basic question, and the host exclaimed, "You can talk! Oh my God, gentlemen and ladies, he can talk!" They all applauded. As I got into politics, the same thing happened.

If you ever find yourself in a similar situation with people in positions of power or influence to whom you must sell your vision, recognize that they are presenting you with a fantastic chance. When you're different, when you're one-of-a-kind, and no one has ever dealt with someone like you before, people will vastly underestimate what you're capable of. Don't allow your ego to get the best of you. You should not correct them. You may use their doubts and underestimate them to effortlessly bridge the conversation, interview, or negotiation to whatever you want to talk about if you can stay focused on winning and achieving your goals. Bridging is a communication technique that anyone can use to gain control of a hostile discussion or avoid answering a question you don't want to answer by redirecting the conversation to a topic that better serves your agenda rather than the agenda of the person on the other side of the microphone or the negotiating table. I originally learned about bridging from the late Jim Lorimer, a lifelong friend, mentor, and Arnold Sports Festival business partner. Jim was an attorney, an FBI agent, a municipal politician, an insurance executive, a law professor, and the author of several law textbooks. The man knew how to respond to the question he wanted to answer, not the one you posed. Jim's argument was that no one who puts a microphone in front of your face and bombards you with questions is doing you a favour. They have their own objective, whether it's filling up column inches, coaxing out a provocative statement to gain more attention, or, in some situations, simply making you look like an idiot. You owe nothing to them. You certainly do not owe them the response they believe they are entitled to. This is your time as well as theirs. This is your chance to tell your tale and sell your vision just as much as it is theirs to create whatever narrative attracts them. So use that time and opportunity to shift the conversation away from what they want to hear and toward what you need to say to achieve your objectives. Jim told me that the best approach to do this is to first listen to the question being asked and then begin your response by accepting the premise of the question in order to build common ground with the questioner. After you've made them feel a little more at ease, you instantly pivot to reframe the question and answer whatever you want. I'll demonstrate.

"Arnold, you've never run for office at any level before." What makes you think you're capable of running the country's largest state?"

"That's a great question, but you know a better question is how can the greatest state in the country afford to continue down this road with the same kind of politicians who got us into this mess in the first place?"

It's similar to judo. You don't want to fight the momentum of those who are dismissive of you. Instead, you want to turn their momentum against them by seizing it, pivoting, and hurling their asses out of the ring. You want to throw their nonsense directly into the rubbish can. Without realising it, critics and journalists had succeeded in making bridging my agenda feel like a stroll in the park with their patronising questions building up to the discussion. They did nothing except lower the bar for what voters needed to hear from me in order to purchase me as a legitimate gubernatorial candidate with their basic narrative about my candidacy. By the night of the debate, I felt like all I had to do was show up sober and alert to meet the media's expectations for my performance. I decided to outdo myself. As the debate devolved into chaos and candidates began sniping at one another from either side of the strangely V-shaped dais, I focused on bridging every leading question from the moderator and every snarky comment from one of my opponents to talking about leadership, rattling off a few policy ideas, and then ripping off a few timely jokes for good measure. When I told Arianna Huffington that I had a part for her in Terminator 4, she was furious. She enjoyed it almost as much as Cruz Bustamante enjoyed being referred to as "Gray Davis: The Sequel." Throughout the night, my goal was to demonstrate that I was a good listener, an effective communicator, a fighter, and a patriot who thought it was time to give back by putting Californians first. Essentially, I intended to demonstrate to voters that I was the polar opposite of everyone and everything that had led to the recall in the first place. I was successful.

I had about 25% support in the polls the day before the debate. Just two weeks later, on Election Day, I received 48.6 percent of the vote—a total of 4.2 million ballots. More than 300,000 more votes than the runners-up and third-place finishers combined. Nobody could believe it. Following the election, media sites around the country ran headlines about my rapid rise. Except that I hadn't risen anyplace. I'd spent hours preparing, rehearsing the jokes I'd sprinkled in, going over my talking points until I knew them by heart, and I'd wrapped my arms around all of the policies I believed were most vital for California's future. In a nutshell, I was exactly where I had always been. Everyone else eventually got on my level when they realised what they had been underestimating the entire time.

Be Yourself, Own the Story, Reap the Rewards

The date was November 10, 2005. I'd been governor of California for two years, and I'd just gotten my a$$ handed to me in a special election that I'd called against the advice of many people, in order to offer four policy ideas to the public that I couldn't advance by working with the legislature. As I told the reporters gathered at the Capitol for this press conference right after the election, when I want to do something, something I truly believe in, I can be aggressive and impatient.

It was a difficult campaign. We spent a significant amount of money. We had a lot of fights, both publicly and personally. The news coverage of these battles was hostile. By the conclusion, my approval rating had dropped to 33%, which was lower than George W. Bush's in California, which is saying something. With my reelection campaign just around the horizon, pundits projected that I had doomed the rest of my governorship by misreading the political terrain.

Californians had elected me to upend the established quo and take on the Capitol's special interests. At the ballot box, they were saying to me, "Hey, Schnitzel, we sent you up there to do the work, not to bring the work to us." Speaking to California's 35 million inhabitants through the reporters in the room and the television cameras behind them, I made it obvious that I had heard their message loud and clear.

"I take full responsibility for this election," that's what I said. "I accept complete responsibility for its failure." "The onus is on me."

My team was standing behind me. I'd spent the previous day debriefing with them, diving into returns, and having a much better sense of the numbers. They were depressed. Three of the four measures were defeated by double digits. This was not my team's fault, and I made that clear to everyone. I'd spent hours in a closed-door breakfast meeting with the Senate and Assembly leadership before coming out to speak to the press. I ordered the crow with a side of "I told you so," and I ate my fair portion of both. When I announced the election five months ago, I did not anticipate myself standing up to the microphone to accept responsibility for the outcome.

For a moment, put yourself in my shoes. How do you imagine that must have felt? Standing in front of my opponents as well as those who believed in me the most, in front of the entire state, if not the entire country, and saying that I'd gotten it wrong. That I'd made a blunder. I'd irritated a lot of people, and it was entirely my responsibility, not anyone else's.

You might be surprised, but it wasn't all that difficult. Taking responsibility for the outcome of an entire election—or, to be honest, its mere existence—was unusual for a high-profile politician. However, it was not unique to me. I don't run from accountability. I am responsible for who I am and what I do, including my accomplishments and failings. This was only the most recent example of facing a contentious decision or an uncomfortable truth and owning it. During the recall effort, I was asked about my previous marijuana use. Unlike some other politicians, I did not play games. "Yes," I responded, "and I inhaled." When a journalist unearthed a bizarre video I didn't try to explain or deny what I'd done for Playboy during Carnival in the early 1980s. I simply stated, "That was such a great time." Because it was true.

Why would you lie? What is the purpose of that? One of the primary reasons people voted for me was that I am not your average politician with a false perfect veneer. I'm just a regular person who enjoys having fun. Why pretend that the events that brought me to where I am and shaped me into the person I am did not occur? All I'd be doing is placing myself in a position to sell someone else's story.

This is something you should consider. What is the point of pretending to be someone you aren't? Of concealing your genuine narrative and allowing someone else to convey it? What do you believe the eventual result will be? I assure you, it's not good. Accept yourself for who you are! Take charge of your narrative! Even if you don't agree with it. Even if it's horrible and you're embarrassed about it. Even if you mean good, running away and hiding from your past, denying your tale and trying to sell a different one, makes you look like a con artist. Worse yet, a politician.

Taking responsibility for the election was an obvious choice in that context. It was also the correct and smart thing to do if I still wanted to realise the vision I had for California when I decided to run for governor in the first place. If I didn't stand up and explain what happened, why it happened, who was responsible, how things would be different, and where we would go from there—if I didn't fill this bucket first—then my opponents and all those journalists in front of me would explain it themselves, twisting my ideas and using the words of others whose vision was likely not aligned with mine.

So, what precisely happened? Ironically, I didn't do a good job of telling the narrative. I didn't sell the value proposition of each initiative I put on the ballot, and I didn't tie them to my vision for California well enough. I failed to articulate the concerns at the heart of each ballot item effectively. What went wrong? My rhetoric was overly forceful. My explanations were far too technical. I expected people would understand what I was saying or would learn because these were major topics that affected their life.

I'd completely forgotten who my customers were. The moderate and undecided voters I needed to persuade saw no connection between these concerns and their lives. Tenure of teachers. State spending caps. Political contributions and union dues. Even redistricting reform fell flat with them. In that case, it was because I focused on the mechanics of redrawing district boundaries rather than the philosophy behind why we were attempting to change them in the first place: to take power away from politicians so that the state's districts more accurately reflected how people lived.

Simply put, I'd loaded the bucket with crap that most Californians didn't want to wade through at the time. It was my fault, and I would never do that to the people again. I would also not force them to arbitrate disagreements between my office and the legislature. Going forward, we'd figure out what areas we might collaborate on and then focus on enacting laws in those areas. This was the promise I made to the press at the press conference, and it was fulfilled.

Do you still not believe me? Let me tell you about the following several years. The legislature and I collaborated like never before during the next year. We had incredible, productive sessions that resulted in Assembly Bill (AB) 32, a landmark environmental bill aimed at reducing greenhouse gas emissions by 25% by 2020; Senate Bill (SB) 1, the most ambitious solar energy policy ever attempted, dubbed the "million solar roofs" initiative; and a $50 billion infrastructure package to rebuild California's roads, highways, bridges, classrooms, levees, affordable housing, and rail systems, among other things. And do you know what the key was to convincing the public to support the infrastructure package? After learning my lesson in 2005, I rarely used technical terms such as "infrastructure" by itself. Instead, I spoke on the need to repair our existing roads and construct new ones so that parents are not trapped in traffic for lengthy periods of time and miss their children's soccer practices as frequently. I mentioned repairing bridges and train lines so that people could buy what they needed when they needed it. I told California voters that the faster we transported people and things, the greater our economic power. Instead than talking about the corruption and unfairness in our state's redistricting laws, I told voters that I intended to take power away from politicians and give it to the people. I recounted my narrative in a way that was relevant to the lives of the people I was attempting to sell to. Then, in June 2006, I was re-elected governor with a higher percentage of the vote (55.9 percent) and a higher total number of votes (4.85 million) than in 2003.

Consider what would have happened if I hadn't held that post-election press conference. If, instead, I'd gone inside my office and refused to speak to anyone or make any comments. Refusing to accept responsibility and apologise for my blunder would have made me a typical politician, which was the exact reverse of what voters stated they wanted when they elected me. Worse, it would have given every single media outlet covering the election free rein to fill the public's bucket with their own version of events. The stories would have undoubtedly been horrifying. The story might have gone something like this: "It only took Arnold two years to become part of the problem—another heartless, arrogant, out-of-touch politician." I can already see the snide headlines: Arnold is fired by voters. The most recent activity was nil. Goodbye, Mr. President.

Except that none of those headlines were true. The news reports that followed had little in common with those about the 2003 gubernatorial debate and recall election. There was no sensation of surprise or astonishment. They weren't full of nonsense or gossip. In fact, the stories in 2005 were tedious. Matter-of-fact. It's almost boring. They were standard political criticism and analysis. Because I had made the decision, like you do, to own my tale, to write it myself, in my own words.

This is something you should consider. What is the point of pretending to be someone you aren't? Of concealing your genuine narrative and allowing someone else to convey it? What do you believe the eventual result will be? I assure you, it's not good. Accept yourself for who you are! Take charge of your narrative! Even if you don't agree with it. Even if it's horrible and you're embarrassed about it. Even if you mean good, running away and hiding from your past, denying your tale and trying to sell a different one, makes you look like a con artist. Worse yet, a politician.

Taking responsibility for the election was an obvious choice in that context. It was also the correct and smart thing to do if I still wanted to realise the vision I had for California when I decided to run for governor in the first place. If I didn't stand up and explain what happened, why it happened, who was responsible, how things would be different, and where we would go from there—if I didn't fill this bucket first—then my opponents and all those journalists in front of me would explain it themselves, twisting my ideas and using the words of others whose vision was likely not aligned with mine.

So, what precisely happened? Ironically, I didn't do a good job of telling the narrative. I didn't sell the value proposition of each initiative I put on the ballot, and I didn't tie them to my vision for California well enough. I failed to articulate the concerns at the heart of each ballot item effectively. What went wrong? My rhetoric was overly forceful. My explanations were far too technical. I expected people would understand what I was saying or would learn because these were major topics that affected their life.

I'd completely forgotten who my customers were. The moderate and undecided voters I needed to persuade saw no connection between these concerns and their lives. Tenure of teachers. State spending caps. Political contributions and union dues. Even redistricting reform fell flat with them. In that case, it was because I focused on the mechanics of redrawing district boundaries rather than the philosophy behind why we were attempting to change them in the first place: to take power away from politicians so that the state's districts more accurately reflected how people lived.

Simply put, I'd loaded the bucket with crap that most Californians didn't want to wade through at the time. It was my fault, and I would never do that to the people again. I would also not force them to arbitrate disagreements between my office and the legislature. Going forward, we'd figure out what areas we might collaborate on and then focus on enacting laws in those areas. This was the promise I made to the press at the press conference, and it was fulfilled.

Do you still not believe me? Let me tell you about the following several years. The legislature and I collaborated like never before during the next year. We had incredible, productive sessions that resulted in Assembly Bill (AB) 32, a landmark environmental bill aimed at reducing greenhouse gas emissions by 25% by 2020; Senate Bill (SB) 1, the most ambitious solar energy policy ever attempted, dubbed the "million solar roofs" initiative; and a $50 billion infrastructure package to rebuild California's roads, highways, bridges, classrooms, levees, affordable housing, and rail systems, among other things. And do you know what the key was to convincing the public to support the infrastructure package? After learning my lesson in 2005, I rarely used technical terms such as "infrastructure" by itself. Instead, I spoke on the need to repair our existing roads and construct new ones so that parents are not trapped in traffic for lengthy periods of time and miss their children's soccer practices as frequently. I mentioned repairing bridges and train lines so that people could buy what they needed when they needed it. I told California voters that the faster we transported people and things, the greater our economic power. Instead than talking about the corruption and unfairness in our state's redistricting laws, I told voters that I intended to take power away from politicians and give it to the people. I recounted my narrative in a way that was relevant to the lives of the people I was attempting to sell to. Then, in June 2006, I was re-elected governor with a higher percentage of the vote (55.9 percent) and a higher total number of votes (4.85 million) than in 2003.

Consider what would have happened if I hadn't held that post-election press conference. If, instead, I'd gone inside my office and refused to speak to anyone or make any comments. Refusing to accept responsibility and apologise for my blunder would have made me a typical politician, which was the exact reverse of what voters stated they wanted when they elected me. Worse, it would have given every single media outlet covering the election free rein to fill the public's bucket with their own version of events. The stories would have undoubtedly been horrifying. The story might have gone something like this: "It only took Arnold two years to become part of the problem—another heartless, arrogant, out-of-touch politician." I can already see the snide headlines: Arnold is fired by voters. The most recent activity was nil. Goodbye, Mr. President.

Except that none of those headlines were true. The news reports that followed had little in common with those about the 2003 gubernatorial debate and recall election. There was no sensation of surprise or astonishment. They weren't full of nonsense or gossip. In fact, the stories in 2005 were tedious. Matter-of-fact. It's almost boring. They were standard political criticism and analysis. Because I had made the decision, like you do, to own my tale, to write it myself, in my own words.

CHAPTER 5

SHIFT GEARS

In March 2020, like most people, I was confined at home, hooked to my television, watching the news about the deadly epidemic that was spreading the globe and had just shut down most of America. All we heard from the president of the United States and the governor of California, where I live, in the early days of the pandemic was that we didn't have enough ventilators, masks, and other personal protective equipment (PPE) for hospital workers and first responders. We had some strategic stockpiles, they said, but they'd be gone in no time, and it could take weeks, if not months, to obtain additional PPE to meet the escalating demand. There was no set schedule for ventilators.

What I was hearing was unbelievable. To me, this was insane. The United States is the world's third most populous country and the world's largest economy. What do you mean there aren't enough masks? There isn't a chance.

I called a few hospitals in Los Angeles where I'd had interactions as a patient or a politician over the years. I contacted UCLA Medical Center, Cedars-Sinai Medical Center, Martin Luther King Jr. Community Hospital, USC's Keck Hospital, and Santa Monica Medical Center. I inquired of the administrators at each location how things were going. They were all having a difficult time obtaining PPE. Several hospitals already had their physicians and nurses take their masks home at night to wash and reuse for the next shift. The other hospitals were almost there, but they hoped the state would come through before they arrived.

This was quite aggravating to me. During an epidemic of avian flu in Asia in 2006, I contributed more than $200 million to the Health Surge Capacity Initiative, a strategic reserve of medical supplies and equipment for the state of California in case of a pandemic like this. It held fifty million N95 masks and nearly two hundred ventilators, as well as all the equipment needed to establish football field-sized mobile hospitals and the funds required to keep the stockpile operational. But, five years later, during a financial shortage, my successor ceased funding the stockpile to save a few million dollars every year. Because no one was given more money to maintain the masks and ventilators, they eventually became unusable, even those donated to local hospitals.

Our strategic reserve would have easily covered all of these hospitals this early in the pandemic. And here we were, with hospital managers in the country's second largest city turning to the leadership of the country's largest state, who were looking to the leadership of the world's richest country—and no one knew what to do. It's no surprise that people despise politicians. Didn't any of them know about the open market? I told myself to go to Alibaba.com and order ten million masks from a slew of Chinese firms. Call one of those large logistics businesses whose main business is sourcing and transporting items like masks all over the world.

The incompetence was driving me insane. Nonetheless, I made no public statements or called out any of these officials. For one thing, I'd been in their position, and I understood that crisis situations with seemingly easy solutions are always more convoluted than they appear. But, more significantly, I have a rule: never complain about a situation unless you're willing to do anything to improve it. If you notice an issue and don't bring a viable solution to the table, I don't want to hear about how horrible it is. If it hasn't spurred you to try to solve it, it can't be that bad.

And when has complaining ever helped someone get closer to their goals? You strive to make a dream a reality, not complain it into existence. Furthermore, hardships and adversity are a typical part of everyone's journey. Whatever your vision is, you will face challenges. These are trying times. Things that irritate you to no end. You must learn how to deal with these situations. You must practise shifting gears and finding the positive in situations. You must know how to reframe your failures and comprehend the risks you are taking. Confronting problems rather than complaining about them allows you to practise all of these abilities.

In my case, with the mask shortage, I realised that shifting gears— from bitching to Lulu and Whiskey (my donkey and miniature horse) while watching the news on my patio to solving the problem that these jackass politicians had created—would actually allow me to carry out my vision for this phase of my life, which is to help as many people as possible.

I dialled my chief of staff's number. His wife worked for one of the shipping companies I mentioned earlier. "Call her," I told her, "see if there's something we can do to help these people."

We called someone that afternoon, and, to our surprise, the logistics business, Flexport, was already working with someone who was attempting to fix this problem as part of a fundraising campaign called the Frontline Responders Fund. The Flexport guy informed us that they'd put some money in, but if we wanted to join them, that would be excellent, because they had a line on millions of masks and other forms of PPE in China that were going north. The only question was how many millions we would spend.

My immediate impression was, "How does the president, governor, or any of our senators not know about this?" You'd think they'd want to pretend they were paying attention instead of being up their asses. But I stopped myself. There was no time for grumbling. I couldn't let my dissatisfaction with the system's failure prevent me from contributing to the answer to this problem.

My next thought was, "How quickly can I get a million dollars for these people?" Then, how quickly can we send masks to each of the area hospitals with which I'd been in contact? Flexport stated that they would be on the ground in the United States in three days, with boxes of PPE designated for each facility. I called my office right away and told them to contribute a million dollars to the Frontline Responders Fund that day. By the end of the week, each of the containers containing hundreds of thousands of masks was on its way to hospitals.

Shift Gears and Find the Positive

Only recently have social scientists fully comprehended why we appear to respond more strongly to negative stimuli than to positive stimuli. We click on negative photos and news stories more than favourable ones. We expend more energy worrying about unfavourable outcomes than hoping for pleasant outcomes. We even have more words to express negative emotions than pleasant feelings. This behaviour is known as "negativity bias," and experts believe it is a type of survival strategy. Our ancestors who worried less about what could make them sick or kill them and focused more on pleasant experiences probably got weeded out disproportionately, so over the last six million years of human evolution we have adapted to be more sensitive to negative influences than positive ones. We have numerous prejudices from our distant past that are no longer as useful as they once were, and this is without a doubt one of them.

When you think about it, it makes a lot of sense, but to be honest, I have no use for any of it in my life. Focusing on all of that negativity is a waste of time for me because I don't just want to survive; I want to thrive, and I want you to thrive as well. That is why I believe we must all improve our ability to embrace our circumstances and adjust our viewpoint toward finding the positive in whatever situation we find ourselves in.

I understand that this is more difficult for some than others. I'm fortunate; I've always been this way for as long as I can remember. All of my friends would tell you that one of my most distinguishing characteristics is my ability to find joy in everything I do. Simply being positive has improved my life. I know it can improve your life as well. It might even save it one day. Any reputable oncologist will tell you that if you show them a patient with a positive mindset, they will show you a patient with a positive prognosis. I know it seems like fairy-tale thinking, but cancer doctors know better than anybody that if you believe you have no control over your situation, you are correct. If you believe you can overcome them and thrive as a result of them, you are correct.

I often consider how different my life may have been if I hadn't been a happy person, if I had reacted differently to my childhood in Thal. I didn't have a hot shower or regular meat in my diet until I joined the army as a teenager. My regular morning routine included getting water and cutting firewood, which was hard in the winter and won me zero compassion from my father, who had been through much worse as a child. There were no free passes in Gustav Schwarzenegger's home. There will be no complimentary dinners either. Every morning, I had to do two hundred knee bends just to "earn" my meal. Nothing works up an appetite like bobbing up and down like a pogo stick on an empty stomach.

The drudgery of all that discomfort and thankless effort could have destroyed my soul or made the images of America I saw in periodicals and newsreels seem impossibly far away. It could have numbed my impulse to scan the horizon. I wasn't getting any encouragement at home to think about life beyond the hills of southeastern Austria. When I got out of the service, I had a good position with the police waiting for me. Others should be so fortunate, my father thought. He also didn't understand or approve of my interest in bodybuilding. He believed it was egotistical and selfish. "Why don't you chop some wood instead," he'll suggest, "you can get big and strong that way and at least then you will have done something for somebody else." Then there were the times when he would come home intoxicated from work and hit us. Those evenings were quite difficult.

I might have easily become engrossed in all of that, but I opted to focus on the positive. I've always made that choice, knowing that on the vast majority of days, my father was a fantastic parent and my mother was the best mother. That life wasn't thrilling or very comfortable, at least not by modern standards, but it was a nice existence. A life in which I learnt a lot and discovered my passion, my purpose, and my first mentors.

Even with the indisputably horrible things, I prefer to remember that they were a significant part of what motivated me to flee, to achieve, to become the person I am today. If my childhood had been a tiny bit better, you might not be holding this book right now. And if it had been a little bit worse, you could not be holding it either, because I could have fallen down the same rabbit hole of alcoholism that my brother fell down, which eventually lost him his life in a drunk-driving accident in 1971.

I owe a great deal to my upbringing. I was built for it, and it made me. Without each of those events, I would not be who I am now. Amor fati is a Stoic phrase for this. Fate's love. "Do not seek for things to happen the way you want them to," urged Epictetus, the famous Stoic philosopher and former slave. "Rather, wish for what happens to happen the way it does." Then you'll be content."

This is also mentioned by Nietzsche. "My formula for human greatness is amor fati: that one wants nothing to be different, not forward, not backward, not in all eternity," he says. "Love what is necessary, not just bear it."

It takes some effort to get here. It's counterintuitive to look adversity or unhappiness in the face and say, "Yes, this is exactly what I needed." This is just what I desired. This is fantastic." Ironically, our innate negativity bias draws us to all the horrible stuff going on in the world, but it also makes us want to flee, ignore, and turn a blind eye to difficulties when it arrives at our door. And if it doesn't work, we'll just whine. It can happen to anyone. We're all guilty of it all the time, with large things and small things alike.

When I'm in a bad position and the impulse to whine and moan arises within me, I stop, take a deep breath, and tell myself that it's time to change gears. I'll literally speak to myself and remind myself to look for the good in my situation.

In March 2018, I was in one of the worst situations imaginable: the postoperative intensive care unit after what was meant to be a "minimally invasive" valve-replacement treatment evolved into full-fledged open-heart surgery. The surgeon mistakenly blew through my heart wall at some point during the procedure, so they had to swiftly break my chest open and fix the damage while replacing the valve the old-fashioned manner.

If everything had gone regularly, I would have been out of the hospital in a couple of days and up and about as if nothing had occurred a couple of days later. That is why I chose to have the operation at the time I did. I'd been in a meeting a few weeks earlier with a ninety-year-old man who'd had the same treatment only a few days before and looked like he'd just returned from a spa. This would be ideal timing, I reasoned. I knew I needed to replace the valve, which had a 10 to twelve year lifespan. It was first implanted in 1997, when I had my first heart surgery to repair a bicuspid aortic valve, a type of prenatal heart defect that can cause no symptoms for some people their entire lives but can be fatal for others, as it would be for my mother the following year. I'd put off the replacement operation because I was too busy and because, according to what I'd heard, heart surgery was still a pain. Now I was told that it was almost like arthroscopic surgery, which was exactly what I needed because I had to be in Budapest in a few months to begin filming on Terminator: Dark Fate. The goal was to get the surgery, then recuperate for a week before returning to the gym to prepare for filming.

Then I awoke. A breathing tube was forced down my throat, and the doctor was standing over me. "I'm sorry, Arnold," the doctor apologised, "but there were complications." We had no choice except to open you up."

As the doctor presented the scenario, numerous ideas and emotions raced through my mind. I was terrified because they had almost killed me. I was furious since this was going to be a significant issue for production. I was frustrated because I remembered how long it took me to recover from my first open-heart surgery, and I was twenty-one years younger at the time. It was also a little depressing when the doctors informed me I'd be in the hospital for at least a week and that I wouldn't be able to lift anything for at least a month after I was released. And they wouldn't let me leave until I could take deep breaths without straining my lungs, walk without assistance, and take a shit—or, as I called it, "declaring victory"—without assistance getting into and out of the bathroom.

I allowed myself to feel all of those feelings, but when the physicians eventually left the room, I told myself, "OK, Arnold, this isn't what you would have preferred, but you're alive." Let's change gears here. You now have a goal: get out of here. And you have a mission: complete all of your exercises and acquire the results that will allow you to be released. It's time to get started."

I pressed the call button beside my bed. I asked a nurse to erase a part of the dry erase board on the wall across from me and write "Breathing" and "Walking" at the top with a line underneath them. I instructed her to add a tally mark to the board every time I finished a session of the breathing exercises or performed some walking and arrived at my destination—the end of the corridor, around the nurses' station, to the elevators. I planned to handle this like my former workouts in Graz, as well as my film and speech preparation. This was a functional system. This was something I was familiar with. It also allowed me to visually track my development, which provided me confidence and motivation. It also meant I didn't have to worry about it, which allowed me to focus all of my mental attention on ignoring the burning in my lungs as I inhaled and exhaled into breathing equipment that resembled a cross between a chemical beaker and a cat toy. I was able to concentrate on firing my leg, arm, and back muscles as I walked down the hospital corridors, first with a walker, then with a cane, and finally just with the rolling IV stand that carried the bag connected to the drainage tube sticking out of my chest.

I "declared victory" a day sooner than predicted, and I was released from the ICU after only six days. I was in my home gym a month after the surgery—maybe a day or two earlier, if I'm being honest— with the IV stand next to me and the drainage tube still protruding out of my chest draped over the bar of the lat pulldown machine, doing a bunch of reps with no weight to wake up my muscles. Within a month, I was adding weight to every lift—twenty pounds, forty pounds, sixty pounds, and so on. A month later, I was on a plane to Budapest to begin production on time.

I don't tell this tale frequently, but when I do, many people wonder if I ever sued the physicians for nearly killing me on the table. This usually surprises me because I never considered it before. Mistakes occur. In reality, I was aware that mistakes could occur with this type of surgery. The actor Bill Paxton died the year before from complications following a similar valve-replacement treatment at the same hospital. That's why I told the hospital authorities that I wouldn't undertake the surgery there unless the open-heart surgery team was there. Aside from that, and despite the fact that I had planned for this possibility, these doctors are only human. They tried their hardest. Not to mention that they saved my life! What is the point of suing them? It makes no difference what happened. Other than the lawyers, who would benefit? What good could any of us take away from that experience if it resulted in a lawsuit?

Viktor Frankl, a famous Austrian psychologist and Holocaust survivor, felt that, while we cannot control many events in our life, we can always influence how we feel and what we do about them. So, here are some inquiries for you: How many hours do you believe you waste each week moaning about things that are out of your control? How much time do you waste worrying about things that you can't reasonably forecast or prevent? How much time do you give yourself each day to read articles and social media posts that irritate you but have nothing to do with your life? How many times have you become enraged in traffic and brought that negative mood into the office, the classroom, or your front door at home? We just discussed how busy your everyday schedule is and how you must protect the limited hours you have each week to work on reaching your vision. By succumbing to negativity, you allow it to steal time from you, your dream, and the people closest to you whom it is your responsibility to lead—whether it's your family, your intramural sports team, your work project group, your unit, or whatever it is.

But you can go back in time! It can be repurposed. You can make it useful. You have the ability to transform a negative situation into a great experience. It all begins with catching yourself whenever you begin to complain, then talking yourself into shifting gears and searching for the good in things. If you can choose joy over jealousy, happiness over hatred, love over resentment, and positive over negativity, you will have the ability to make the best of any circumstance, even one that appears to be a failure.

Reframe Failure

People constantly approach me and say, "Arnold, I didn't meet the goal I set for myself; what should I do?" Or they remark, "Arnold, I asked my crush out and she said no." Or might it be that "I failed this week to get the promotion I wanted, what do I do now?"

My response is straightforward: Learn from your mistakes before declaring, "I'll be back."

That is frequently all the counsel folks require. They're just terrified, or maybe desperate, and they need some motivation to get back on track. Others, on the other hand, want to whine that life is unfair because the thing they wanted so badly didn't happen exactly when they wanted it to, and it hurts too much to consider the idea that they didn't put in enough effort to obtain their desired outcome. I don't say this with condemnation; I've been there. I was depressed and inconsolable after losing against Frank Zane in 1968. After that, I cried all night in my hotel room. It felt like the entire universe had collapsed on me. I wondered why I had come to America in the first place. I was separated from my parents and friends, I didn't understand the language, and I didn't know anyone in Miami. I was all alone. And for what purpose? For second place to a guy who was half my size?

I blamed everything and everyone for my loss. The judging was flawed. The judges favoured Frank, who was an American. Travelling from London and eating poor food in the airport the day before had had a negative impact on my physique and training. The defeat was too hard for me to face in the mirror and confess that perhaps I hadn't done enough to win and that it was my fault. Joe Weider invited me to come out to Los Angeles the next morning for breakfast. Only after working out with the guys at Gold's for a few weeks could I recognize the difference between Frank and me, and confess that he'd won fairly and squarely. I was simply not as well-defined. This was true not only in comparison to Frank, but to practically all of the American men I was working out with. I was bigger and had greater symmetry than them, but they were doing something I wasn't that allowed them to get so cut. I had to figure out what that was and start doing it myself if I wanted to be the best. So, once I'd settled into my new Santa Monica apartment, I invited Frank to stay with me so we could train together and he could teach me a thing or two. He did, however, accept my invitation. He stayed with me for a month, we worked out every day at Gold's, he taught me the workouts he used to get absolutely shredded, and then he never beat me again. Let me make one thing perfectly clear. And this is for anybody who has ever failed, which is every single one of us: failure is not fatal. I know, I know, it's a cliche. But, at this time, every good rhetoric about failure has become a cliché, since we all know it's true. Everyone who has achieved something they are proud of, and who we appreciate as a society, will tell you that they learnt more from their mistakes than their achievements. They will assure you that failing isn't the end of the world. And they are correct.

When viewed correctly, failure is actually the beginning of measured achievement, because failure is only conceivable in situations when you have attempted to accomplish something tough and worthy. When you don't try, you can't fail. In that sense, failure is similar to a status report on your road to purpose. It demonstrates how far you've gone while also reminding you of how far you still have to go and what you need to focus on to get there. It's an opportunity to learn from your mistakes, improve your approach, and return stronger than before. This, like many other things, I learnt in the gym while training for weight-lifting competitions when I was younger. The beauty of weight lifting is that failing is a natural part of the process. We sometimes forget that the whole point of weight lifting is to strain your muscles to failure. It's natural to feel frustrated when you can't squeeze out that last rep or lock out those elbows before lowering the weight, but you have to realise that failure on that particular exercise doesn't mean you've lost. It actually signifies that your workout was effective and that your muscles were completely exhausted. It implies that you accomplished the work.

Failure in the gym does not mean loss; it equals success. It's one of the reasons I've always felt at ease pushing the boundaries in whatever I do. When failing is a good element of the game, it's a lot less frightening to look for the boundaries of your ability—whether that's speaking English, acting in huge movies, or confronting big societal problems—and then to grow beyond them after you've found them. The only way to accomplish so, however, is to repeatedly put yourself to the test and risk failing.

Weight-lifting tournaments are structured in this manner. A traditional meet includes three lifts. Your initial lift is a foregone conclusion. It's a weight you've done before and are familiar with.

The goal is to get your feet under you, get the butterflies out of your stomach, and make sure you've put one good lift on the board. Your second lift is a bit of a stretch: you lift something close to your personal record weight in order to put some pressure on your competition. Maybe you don't win, but at least you'll know you've reached your previous limit. You're on your third attempt to raise a weight you've never lifted before. You're attempting to break new ground, both for yourself as a weight lifter and for the sport as a whole. This is the last lift where records are broken and victories are claimed. It is also where failure occurs most frequently. As a weight lifter, I failed 10 separate final lifts to bench press 500 pounds, which was nearly unheard of at the time. Benching 500 pounds became simpler after I finally achieved it, and it led me on a path to eventually bench 525 pounds.

That third lift is a microcosm of pursuing your dreams in the real world. It will be challenging and strange. People will be watching and judging, and failure is not out of the question. In many ways, failure is unavoidable. But when it comes to realising your vision, it's not failing that you should be concerned about; it's giving up. Failure has never killed a dream; quitting kills every dream it comes into contact with. No one who has set a world record, created a successful business, achieved the highest score on a video game, or accomplished something challenging that they cared about has ever quit. They got to where they are after a series of failures. They rose to the summit of their profession, produced game-changing innovations, and realised their wildest dreams because they persevered in the face of failure and actively paid attention to the lessons that failure is supposed to teach us.

Consider the chemist who developed the lubricating spray WD-40. WD-40 is an abbreviation for "Water Displacement, 40th Formula." Because his previous thirty-nine attempts at the formula had failed, it was given that name in the chemist's lab book. He learned from each of his mistakes and succeeded on the forty-fifth attempt.

Thomas Edison is famous for learning from his mistakes. So much so that he refused to call them failures at all. Edison and his colleagues, for example, were attempting to construct a nickel-iron battery in the

1890s. Over the course of six months, they developed almost nine thousand prototypes, all of which failed. When one of his assistants remarked that they hadn't produced any promising results, Edison said, "Why, man, I have gotten a lot of results!" I know a thousand things that will not work." This was Edison's perspective on the world as a scientist, inventor, and businessman. It was Edison's optimistic outlook, his genius reframe of failure, that led to the development of the lightbulb barely a decade earlier, as well as the thousand other patents he had by the time he died.

As you consider what you want to do or the impact you want to make in the world, keep in mind that your duty is neither to avoid nor to seek failure. Your task is to work your tail off in pursuit of your vision—yours and no one else's—and to accept the inevitable failure. Failure, like those last hard reps in the gym, indicates that you're one step closer to your objective. Or, as Edison would say, which way it should not go. This is why failure is worth the risk and should be embraced: it teaches you what doesn't work and directs you toward what works.

Personally, I credit a number of my triumphs as governor, including my reelection, to having learned from the failure of the 2005 special election and then applying those lessons to direct my next steps. The voters informed me it was a tremendous mistake to bring my issues with the legislature to their doorstep. They informed me that speaking like a technocrat or a policy wonk, rather than like the ordinary person and non-politician they'd chosen, wouldn't work for them. Californians told me that if I wanted to get anything done, I couldn't adopt those approaches again. They were voting for explanations in plain English instead, and they were pointing me in the direction of my opponents, telling me that the solution to my problem was there.

So I paid attention to them. Following the election, I flew the leadership of both parties, from both houses of the legislature, to Washington, DC, to meet with California's full congressional delegation and discuss how to better serve the people. We sat in close quarters, forty thousand feet above America, for five hours on each trip, talking not as political opponents, but as public servants with a common cause: helping Californians live happier, richer, healthier lives. The broad strokes of a number of bipartisan efforts had been sketched out by the time we returned home a few days later.

Had I chosen to whine about the outcome of the special election, had I vilified my opponents instead of defying political convention and taking responsibility for my policy failures, there's very little chance that any of this gets done, and there's no way in hell that I'll be reelected a year later. It's not an exaggeration to suggest that the triumphs I've had were the direct result of learning from failure.

Break the Rules

In 1972, comedian George Carlin released Class Clown, which included a segment that would go on to become one of the most renowned of all time. It's called "Seven Words You Can Never Say on Television," and it's an extended riff on the seven nasty words that can't be used on American television. We have our own seven dirty words in the Schwarzenegger household: "It's how things have always been done." I see red when I hear such phrases. It irritates me when individuals use them to excuse refusing new things they don't comprehend. But what really irritates me is when the folks doing the new things are told to accept the seven-word status quo and give up. That makes me want to channel my inner "John Matrix in the toolshed."

When pursuing a grand vision, you must expect to encounter opposition. Others who have vision are threatened by others who have not. Their natural reaction is to raise their hands and exclaim, "No! Wait a minute, let's take it easy here." It's not that they believe you can't do it; rather, they believe it shouldn't be done in the first place. They are afraid of new ideas. Large undertakings can be intimidating. They are uneasy among those who want to break the mould or make a splash. They are far more at peace with those who can accept without inquiry that there is simply a way things have always been done. Obviously, I am not one of those folks. I'm guessing you're not one of those folks either. My entire life has been an experiment in doing things in unconventional ways. As a bodybuilder, I did two full workouts every day, not one as most people do. As an actor, I didn't perform little parts in TV shows or films like producers suggested; instead, I focused on starring roles. As a politician, I did not go for municipal council, mayor, or state senator, as the party bosses and kingmakers required; instead, I went straight for the governorship. My goal from the start was to be the best bodybuilder, then the largest star, and finally to help the most people. Not someday, not eventually, but as soon as I was able. My strategy did not include paying dues, climbing an invisible ladder, or waiting for authorization. That didn't sit well with the gatekeepers, power brokers, and status quo guardians I encountered in each of these stages of my life. The fact that I didn't listen to their complaints bothered them more than my readiness to make waves, and I didn't care that it bothered them. This was never more evident than during my governorship. I broke a lot of regulations while in Sacramento, and no one was more furious than my own party members. They responded as if I'd just allowed the fox into the henhouse when I appointed Democrat Susan Kennedy as my chief of staff. One Republican senator was so concerned that he came into my office, sat on the sofa next to my chair, peered around the room like some kind of conspiratorial cartoon villain, and then whispered in my ear that she was a lesbian, just in case I didn't know. As if it were a warning. Of course, I already knew it, but what did it matter?

"But did you know she burned her bra!?" he exclaimed, apparently desperate to persuade me to reconsider.

"So?" I asked. "I didn't need it."

And that was nothing compared to the outrage shown by Republican insiders when half of my judicial nominations were made by Democrats. You'd think I'd desecrated Abraham Lincoln's tomb while cursing Ronald Reagan's name. Appointing judges is one of those areas in politics where most politicians, whether governors or presidents, nearly always choose judges from their own party. I told my team that we were not going to do that. I instructed them to bring me the best candidates available and to delete their party membership from the briefing documents. Why? Because I promised voters that I would be a new sort of public servant, not just another party servant, and that meant hiring the finest individuals for the job. As a result, there were half Democrats and half Republicans. To me, it appears to be fairly and representative. This is a story I gave in 2012 during my speech at the launch of the USC Schwarzenegger Institute, a think tank dedicated to bipartisanship and putting people over politics, whose sole aim is to defy the current quo and violate the norms. I told the crowd how Sacramento party hacks couldn't understand my thinking and couldn't accept it when I ignored them. Then I emphasised that if there was one thing I'd learned from campaigning and running for office, it was that the old way of doing things didn't work. The way things had always been done... it wasn't working any longer. The status quo was not serving the people well (which is why they elected me in the first place), and because my mission was to serve all of the people as best I could, I gleefully broke the regulations that were impeding my vision for development, change, and a better California.

That didn't make my job any easier politically, but after the special election, my mindset was to stop worrying about the status quo and ignore the folks who were fascinated with how things had always been done. Instead, I concentrated on developing working relationships with folks in Sacramento, Washington, and even around the world who were as tired with the old rules as I was and were more interested in getting things done. Everyone else was told to climb on board or get out of the way, and if they didn't, they'd be worked around or run over. Is there a risk in using that strategy to realise your ultimate goal? Possibly. But we're talking about your life and your aspirations here, not theirs. I would argue that risking everything to make your ambitions a reality and create the life you want for yourself is worthwhile.

Risk Is Relative

If you're terrified of risk—which I understand, believe me—it might help to redefine risk in the same way that we've reframed failure. Risk, in my opinion, does not exist. It's not something you can cling to or rely on. Nobody has the same definition of it. It's a shifting objective. It's all made up. It is a perception.

Risk is just the word we give to the judgement that each of us arrives at individually when we weigh the possibilities of success vs the repercussions of failure. If you believe that something is extremely unlikely to succeed and that the implications of failure are quite bad, you will likely conclude that the choice is quite dangerous. If the contrary is true—that success is likely and failure would be very inexpensive—then the choice does not appear to be hazardous at all. Except it's not quite that simple, because there's the possibility of success to consider. If the upside isn't substantial enough, even a small amount of risk isn't worth it. But when it's huge enough, as it frequently is with our ambitions, even something you know is technically highly unsafe might be worth the risk. The reality is that when you want something badly enough and it means enough to you, you have to be willing to grasp for the brass ring and stop caring about danger. You must accept that the cliché is occasionally true: the greater the risk, the greater the profit.

Take, for example, rock climber Alex Honnold. Many people believed he was insane when he achieved the first free solo ascent of El Capitan in Yosemite National Park in 2017. They suspected he had a dying wish. But after the documentary about his ascent won the Oscar a year later, and he became renowned and landed a slew of endorsement deals, you didn't hear as many people raving about how insane he was. Before the fame and fortune, he was a daredevil with a loose screw. He was a thoughtful, seasoned climber before fame and money. A dedicated professional who toured the world and was compensated for spending time outside in nature. He was no longer a detrimental influence; he was an inspiration!

Of course, it was never how Honnold saw it; it was how others perceived it. After seeing the documentary and reading interviews with him, their perceptions of his odds of success shifted dramatically, and their perspectives on the repercussions of failure (injury or death) were tempered by witnessing what the upside of success looked like. He was the same guy he was before any of us knew his name; the only difference was how much we knew about him.

The irony is that, while our impression of his climbing's danger has decreased, his has most likely increased. Not because the chances of a successful climb have diminished (in fact, they have improved with experience), but because the terrible repercussions of failure have increased for him. Beyond the possibility of damage or death, which was always a possibility during his free solo attempts, he now has a wife and kid who adore him, as well as a foundation that depends on him. He now stands to lose even more.

That has always been the fundamental question for me when it comes to risk: What do you have to lose? Because I didn't have much to lose in my early life, my risk tolerance has always been very high, and as a result, I've done a lot of things that people believed were doubtful or impossible. And as I grew older and more accomplished, and began trying new things, I learned how to minimise my risk of failure.

What did I have to lose by spending all those hours in the gym in Graz working on my body, then relocating to Munich to work for a stranger in his gym before finally arriving in America?

What did I have to lose by trying my hand at acting? I would have become a seven-time Mr. Olympia even if I stunk at it and no one wanted to give me another chance. I'd still have Joe Weider on my side, my training books to sell, and my apartment complex to keep me warm.

What did I stand to gain by entering politics? Even if I had lost the recall election, even if I had done terribly in the television debate and disgraced myself, I would still be a movie star with many interests. I would have remained wealthy and famous, able to utilise my wealth and influence to support causes close to my heart. such as the Special Olympics and the After-School All-Stars program.

You could argue that there was my reputation at stake if any of the things I pursued had gone tragically wrong. But that suggests I cared what others thought about the goals I set for myself in life. It presumes that I want or require the approval of some group of individuals in order to pursue my dreams. I've only ever sought acceptance from judges at bodybuilding competitions, moviegoers at the box office, and voters at the polls. And I didn't grumble if I didn't get it, if I lost or failed. Instead, I saw it as a learning opportunity. I returned to the gym, the drawing board, or the briefing books, and I worked hard to improve and become smarter in order to return stronger the following time.

Where is the danger in that? The worst thing that can happen when you attempt to overcome hardship rather than giving up is that you fail again and learn yet another method that does not work. Then you're forced to shift gears, which brings you one step closer to your goal because you're now more likely to be moving in the right direction.

What exactly do you have to lose?

CHAPTER 6

SHUT YOUR MOUTH, OPEN YOUR MIND

Fredi Gerstl was the first adult I informed about my desire of being a champion bodybuilder, and he took me seriously and backed me. Fredi was the father of my friend Karl, with whom I used to train at the Graz gymnasium when I was a teenager. Fredi's tale is incredible. He was Jewish but pretended to be Catholic to avoid the Nazis during WWII, and then he joined the Resistance to help bring them down. After the war, he returned to Graz and became involved in local business, politics, and, especially, the local youth. He and his wife erected a couple of tabakladen, or cigarette and magazine kiosks, on prime real estate between the train station and the main square. They were well located for him to keep a pulse on life in Graz and the surrounding area, which would later assist push his political career to the leadership of Austria's upper chamber of Parliament. I first encountered Fredi in the early 1960s, when he formed a group of us boys for athletic training and outdoor physical activities that taught us to be tough and self-sufficient while simultaneously bonding us like Roman gladiators camped out in the field ready for battle. It was a lot of fun, but there was a catch. During my 2003 campaign for governor, Fredi told a reporter from the Los Angeles Times, "I gathered the young people together for sports, but the condition was they had to listen."

What are you listening to? To everything Fredi was interested in and thought we should know, which was a lot. He didn't lecture us like a professor. At the end of the week, there were no quizzes. He was only sowing seeds. "You might not understand this now," he'd say of some concept that passed most of us by, "but one day you will and you will be glad you know it." I didn't realise it at the time, but Fredi was a Renaissance man. He liked sports, dogs, opera, philosophy, and history, among other things, as I would discover over the course of our fifty-year acquaintance. But it was his passion for learning and his emphasis on being open to new experiences—which I feel is the hallmark of a Renaissance man—that had the most impact on my life and, I'm sure, the lives of many of the other guys.

Fredi became a father figure to us in a way that our own fathers couldn't because he had a vision that they didn't. In my instance, because I was much bigger than the other boys my age, Fredi saw that being a serious bodybuilder had the ability to open doors for me, whereas my father feared it would slam in my face because bodybuilding wasn't serious. Fredi was younger than all of our fathers, and he'd been on the right side of the battle, which I think made it easier for him to keep an open mind as he grew older, because he wasn't overwhelmed with regret or shame as many of our fathers were. When you've battled for and won something you believe in—when you've literally saved the world—I guess it's simpler to recognize the joy and possibility in fresh and lovely things.

Fredi always encouraged all of us lads that exercising our minds was just as vital as training our bodies. He showed us that we can't merely want success, money, fame, and muscles. We, too, must be hungry for information. Being in good shape with a strong, muscular physique will help you live a long, healthy life; it will help you obtain females; it will allow you to accomplish a lot of arduous jobs to take care of your family; and, of course, becoming a bodybuilding champion was important for me. But if we wanted to be successful in everything we decided to do, at any age, and if we wanted to maximise our potential and chances, we needed to have a good head on our shoulders and an active mind. Fredi taught us that the world was the ultimate school, and that we needed to absorb up as much of it as we could. He taught us that being curious was the only way to become the type of sponge that absorbs only the most helpful information. We needed to listen and gaze more than we talked. When we did converse, it was preferable to ask good questions than to make intelligent statements. And we needed to understand that any information we received, no matter where it came from, might be put to use at any time, in service of any number of opportunities, difficulties, or challenges, whether tomorrow or twenty years from now. There was no way to be certain. However, we can be certain that knowledge is power and that information makes you useful.

The World Can Be Your Classroom

Nothing drives me insane as a father, businessman, and public servant more than the American system's attempt to force every child into a four-year degree. Colleges are, of course, vital. A college education is beneficial. But it has its uses. A university is the place to be if you want to be a doctor, engineer, accountant, or architect. There are careers in our world that necessitate a college degree and the associated studies. It all makes sense. We don't want doctors who have never studied chemistry to work in hospitals, and we don't want commercial planes that fly six million people every day to be developed by people who have never sat in a maths class.

What if you don't know what you want to do with your life? Or if you're certain that whatever you want to accomplish won't necessitate a college degree? Is it really worth it to burden yourself or your family with $250,000 in student loan debt? For what purpose? A scrap of paper? That is what many young people's college experience has become. If you ask them why they are going to college, they will tell you it is to acquire a degree. That's like saying you go to work to get to the weekend. What about everything in between? What about the goal?!

This is the missing link in the puzzle. Purpose. Vision. We are not giving young people the time and space they need to find their purpose or establish a vision for themselves. We're not letting the world show children what's possible in their lives. Instead, we take them out of the world when they have the least to lose and the most to gain by doing so, and place them in four-year universities, which are the polar opposite of the actual world.

I am living proof that the best place for young people to learn is in the real world. As part of my occupational training, I learnt how to sell as an apprentice on the floor of a hardware store. While sitting in Fredi's living room, I learned how to think about huge questions. Between the ages of sixteen and twenty-five, every other essential item I learnt and took with me into the remainder of my life was either learned in the gym or practised and improved there. Goal setting, planning, hard effort, perseverance in the face of failure, communication, and the value of helping others—the gym was my laboratory for all of these things. It was my high school, college, and graduate school all rolled into one. When I finally stepped into a real college classroom—and I attended a lot of college classes in the 1970s—it was with a purpose, to help me realise my goal. And I was successful in those classes because I tackled them in the same manner I handled my bodybuilding ambitions. As I have stated, all roads lead back to the gym for me.

And yeah, we are discussing ourselves. We've already discussed how I'm a crazy person when it comes to these things. However, every March, when I walk the floor of the Arnold Sports Festival in Columbus, Ohio, I encounter tens of thousands of people with similar tales. Men and women from all around the world who discovered fitness and subsequently discovered a successful life through fitness. I'm referring to gym owners, firefighters, strongmen, and entrepreneurs who offer fitness clothes, nutritional supplements, recovery drinks, and physical therapy equipment, among other things. The majority of these persons do not have a college diploma. And many of those who are would tell you that they don't apply much of what they learned in college in their day-to-day work. Anyone with the ear of a young person should be aware that there are millions of people out there who have formed a vision for themselves and made happy, successful lives outside of the academic system. They are the plumbers, electricians, furniture refinishers, and carpet cleaners we call when we don't know how to remedy a problem ourselves. They work as general contractors, real estate agents, and photographers, among other things. They're skilled craftspeople who learnt by doing, in real time, in the real world. They are also the glue that ties the economy together.

This is something we should emphasise to our children. We should inform them that they can create their ideal life with a hammer and nails, a comb and scissors, a saw and sandpaper. And we should do so not only for their benefit, but also for our own. We don't have enough individuals doing these tasks in many nations throughout the world. In the United Kingdom and the Eurozone, a shortage of trained personnel has hampered the supply chain in several areas. In the United States, where political leaders are attempting to reintroduce computer chip production, there aren't enough trained workers to construct the structures that will house the manufacturing equipment. This is also not a new issue. That is why, as governor, I made significant investments in vocational and career education. Not only to help tradesmen, but also to let people understand how vital their work is and how we need to motivate more young people to pursue careers in such sectors.

I don't think anyone truly knows why we've ended up here, but I feel a large part of it is that we've been blinded by status, which has made us a closed-minded culture. It's why we respect a person's degree more than the number of satisfied clients they've serviced. It's why we adore stories about entrepreneurship, yet if you work with your hands and own your own business, we call you a small-business owner rather than an entrepreneur. And, ironically, when comparing a "small-business owner" to the type of tech entrepreneur we lionise today (some of whose inventions, by the way, are tearing us apart), the person who works with their hands is more likely to be happier and to have owned their home before the highly educated entrepreneur ever made their first student loan payment. Even the most celebrated dropouts in our culture, such as Bill Gates and Mark Zuckerberg, dropped out of Harvard, not high school or some unknown provincial institution.

Let me tell you about another type of dropout. Mary Shenouda is her name. In Venice, she lives just down the hill from me. Mary is a high-performance private chef for professional athletes, actors, entrepreneurs, and executives who must be at the top of their game at all times, which means she must be at the top of her game as well. She taught herself how to play this game. Mary is a totally self-taught chef and performance specialist.

Since she dropped out of high school in the eleventh grade, Mary has taught herself everything she knows. Instead of going to college, Mary went into technology sales and learned how to sell her ass off, much like I did in the hardware store in Graz when I was her age. She was also really excellent at it. Sales was the first thing she discovered she was particularly excellent at other than tennis, so she pursued it as a prospective profession.

However, after a few years, her attention began to move toward food. It had to happen. Mary had been sick for a long time, almost her entire adolescence, which was one of the reasons she dropped out of high school. She didn't realise she was lactose intolerant, soy intolerant, and gluten intolerant until she was in her early twenties. The regular foods accessible in restaurants and supermarkets were targeting her immune system and causing enormous inflammation. If she ever wanted to feel good in her own skin and eat any of her favourite recipes again, she'd have to find a new way to create them that was compatible with her system.

She did exactly that. During the process, she developed a strong attachment to it. She became an accomplished cook in less time than it takes the average individual to complete culinary school. And it just so happened that the world around her was also going through the paleo diet revolution, as well as the keto revolution and the gluten-free revolution, at the same time. More and more individuals were substituting almond milk or coconut milk (now oat milk) for dairy in their coffee or ice cream. These were the nutritional categories Mary discovered herself studying as she devised nutritious and delectable meals for herself. It wasn't long before Mary recognized she was surrounded by a genuine business opportunity. She grew up in Silicon Valley and was living in the San Francisco Bay Area at the time, so she was surrounded by people who, if they had been in her situation, would have applied to business school right away. But, as a high school dropout, that path was not as readily available to her as it would have been to others. Even if it was, as a seasoned salesperson with a brilliant idea and a rising market, the universe was telling her that the moment had come to seize this opportunity. So she listened.

Mary began referring to herself as the "Paleo Chef," and she learned everything she could about turning her purpose-driven passion into a company. She read books and taught herself how to read medical journal articles. She spoke with former supervisors and specialists in all the sectors she needed to understand. She picked the minds of clients and customers. She observed how other people with no money, like her, created their enterprises from the ground up. She made time for and listened to everybody who offered to help her.

That was in 2012. She has since built her private chef service, as well as a performance food product called Phat Fudge that she developed in conjunction with it, not only into successful businesses that make people better (her clients include NBA champions and Oscar winners), but also into a lifestyle that gives her flexibility and control over her own destiny. She made her concept a reality. All of this from a high school dropout with an open mind and a strong work ethic.

For the record, I do not suggest dropping out of high school. You never know what can take you out of commission or make pursuing your vision impossible, forcing you to take a different, more traditional road for a while. In such circumstances, having a high school graduation is analogous to holding a driver's licence. It doesn't make you more prepared; it simply informs others that you are part of the system and understand how to operate inside it.

That being said, the world is set up for you to do what Mary did with practically anything you are excellent at or any problem you are interested in solving, all without having to think about college if you don't want to. It makes no difference if you want to make gluten-, soy-, and lactose-free cuisine, become a fitness professional, a landscaper, or turn your passion into a side business once you retire.

I know it may appear that I'm picking on college, but that's only because the simplest way to close a person's mind is to make them believe that they can't afford to dream, and that's exactly what college has done to many individuals. If you can stop that happening to you, if you can listen to the world around you and pay attention to what gets you thrilled every morning, you'll realise that it's not all that difficult to find a passion or a purpose to construct a vision around.

Be Curious

I've always been more like the character Julius in Twins than John Matrix in Commando. I'm not some supersoldier who always knows what to do and is always one step ahead of everyone; I'm an honest person who may be a little naive about a few things that others take for granted, but who is generally just hungry to learn about the world.

Curiosity has been a superpower for me as an immigrant, as I'm sure many of you are, and as someone who has shifted between various occupations, like many of you have. It has a strong magnetic field. My curiosity has drawn many fantastic chances to me simply by opening my mind to the wonders of the world around me. It has also brought into my life a plethora of good, intelligent people. The type who enjoys teaching, supporting, and lifting people up. This includes some very exceptional people I've met over the years, many of whom I'm delighted to call friends. Reg Park was among the first, followed by Muhammad Ali, Nelson Mandela, Mikhail Gorbachev, the Dalai Lama, and two successive Popes. Friends refer to me as Forrest Gump since I've met every American president since Lyndon B. Johnson. Unlike Forrest, I didn't end myself in the same room with these renowned people by chance; I met them because I was famous. But because I was intrigued, I got to know them and form ties with them. I questioned them about themselves and their experiences. I sought counsel. Then I paid attention.

People that ask good questions and listen well attract important, intriguing, and influential people. People like to talk to you if you're curious and humble enough to confess that you don't know everything. They wish to assist you. Your curiosity and humility demonstrate that you do not have too much ego to listen to them. They know there's no sense to waste their breath when you're closed-minded. What's the sense of trying to teach you something if you're already certain you know everything?

The ability to listen with patience and humility is a necessary component of curiosity, and it is the key to learning. For thousands of years, some of history's brightest thinkers and philosophers have been preaching to us about this, with statements like "We have two ears and one mouth so that we can listen twice as much as we speak." That concept appears often throughout history. The Bible says, "Let every man be swift to hear, slow to speak." "When you talk, you are only repeating what you already know," says the Dalai Lama. But if you pay attention, you might learn something new." "When people talk, listen completely," Ernest Hemingway advised. The majority of people never listen." "I'm a very strong believer in listening and learning from others," stated the late Justice Ruth Bader Ginsburg.

All of these are just other ways of stating that you don't know as much as you think you do, so keep your mouth shut and your mind open. I learned this lesson the hard way with The Terminator, which I could have easily lost if I'd let my agents and ego dispute with a guy who would go on to become one of the greatest directors of all time.

I first met Jim Cameron in the spring of 1983 over lunch at a Hollywood restaurant to discuss his script for The Terminator, which had been brought to me by a guy named Mike Medavoy, the head of the studio that would eventually make the film. I was about to begin filming the sequel to Conan the Barbarian, and Mike, my agents, and I all agreed that this might be my next project, and that I should play Kyle Reese, the story's hero.

On paper, everything made sense: Kyle Reese was a future soldier sent to save Sarah Connor and, by implication, the entire human race from a technologically superior murdering machine. That is the pinnacle of heroism. Our lunch meeting, on the other hand, was nearly entirely devoted to the Terminator. It was undoubtedly the most fascinating and intriguing figure to me. I had a lot of questions and ideas after reading the script regarding how someone should play a robot that is supposed to look like a human person. Throughout lunch, I loved them all at Jim. I could see from his reaction that the breadth of curiosity in my questions and the depth of interest in my views surprised him. I believe he was expecting to encounter a meathead. He believed that the Terminator was the most crucial figure to nail. We even agreed on some of the precise things the Terminator's actor would need to perform to reflect the fact that he was a machine.

During lunch, Jim became convinced that I should be the Terminator. Or, at the very least, he was certain that I was the Terminator. In my thoughts, I thought I could be, but that wasn't the role I wanted to play, and I told him so. Conan was my name. Conan was a legend. I was supposed to play heroes. My ambition was to become the next big action hero. You don't get there by playing the bad guy. Jim was attentive as I expressed my stance, which he understood. That was just conventional Hollywood wisdom I was referring to.

It was then my turn to listen. Jim's point was that this would not be a typical Hollywood action flick. This narrative involved time travel. There was cutting-edge technology. It was a work of science fiction. In science fiction, the rules are different. Furthermore, the Terminator was not the antagonist. Whoever sent the Terminator from the future was the villain. The Terminator simply... is. We can build the character whatever we want based on how I play it and how he shoots it, Jim explained. That is, assuming I accept the post.

The more I thought about the project that night, the more difficult it seemed to shake the vision of myself as the Terminator. My conversation with Jim was all I could think about. His words rang in my ears. Jim had only done one film before this, but his script was so unique, and he seemed to know exactly what he wanted to do with it, that I couldn't help but be convinced by everything he said as he argued for me to play that character instead of Kyle Reese. Plus, by this point, I'd only appeared in one film. Who was I to say I was smarter?

The next day, I called Jim and told him I'd be there.

My agents were opposed to the move. They stood firm in their opposition to heroes playing villains. I heard them, but I didn't pay attention to them. Instead, I trusted my instincts and followed my curiosity. More importantly, I listened to Jim with an open mind. I paid close attention to him. And that resulted in the most important decision of my career. Not because The Terminator was a hit, albeit that helped my money account. Listening to Jim talk about the Terminator in meetings, then observing how he coached me in rehearsals and on site, proved for me that I could be more than just an action hero. I have the potential to be a movie star. A man in charge.

In 1961, I saw Reg Park on the big screen in Graz and had my first huge vision for my life. It changed dramatically while listening to Jim Cameron over lunch in Venice in 1983, and it drove my decisions for the next two decades. Hemingway was correct. When individuals speak, you should pay attention to them.

Be a Sponge

Being curious and a good listener are important aspects of how to use your interactions with other people to achieve your goals. I don't mean that in a manipulative way, but in a practical sense. People are resources when it comes down to it. But it's only when you learn to absorb what those people say to you, rather than merely letting it pass through one ear and out the other, that you can actually begin to make yourself valuable to others and become a resource yourself.

When I campaigned for governor, people who knew me predicted that I would enjoy campaigning but despise sitting in the governor's office debating policy because I crave action, action, action. People who had never met me felt the same way, but for a different reason. They assumed I was always looking for attention, attention, attention. To some extent, both opinions were correct, but they were also incorrect. They failed to account for the fact that the governorship was the best classroom in the world, and they failed to recognize that I have been a sponge of knowledge and new information my entire life, dating back to my early days studying from Fredi and other bodybuilders.

If I observed someone in the gym trying a new training approach that didn't make sense to me, I wouldn't call them a "forehead" (my friend Bill Drake referred to everyone as a "forehead," indicating they had a low forehead like a Neanderthal). I inquired about it because it might be of assistance to me. Back in the day, when I saw the great Vince Gironda execute the side-lying triceps extension at his gym in North Hollywood, I admit I thought it looked a little Mickey Mouse with the tiny weight he was using. But instead of discounting it because it was girlie or completely ignoring it since Vince did not come from a strong lifting background, I gave it a shot. During my next arm workout, I completed forty sets, which I had discovered was the greatest way to see how a new technique affects my body, and my outside triceps shook the entire next day. I had to ask Vince about the exercise because it was so effective.

What inspired you to create this exercise? What makes this movement more effective than others? How should I incorporate it into my training routine?

My questions fulfilled several functions. If the answers made sense to me, they would dispel any doubts or concerns I had. By being curious, as we just discussed, I demonstrated humility and made myself an ally to Vince, increasing the likelihood that he would reveal other beneficial training strategies. Most importantly, asking good "how" and "why" questions about something you're interested in increases the likelihood of that information sticking in your brain and connecting with other related bits of information—making everything more useful to you when it comes time to put it all to work in service of others.

That's why I loved my position as governor more than any other. It was an opportunity to absorb all of this knowledge about how our society works while also being able to use that knowledge to aid millions of others. One minute, I was discovering that we needed additional prison guards because their working conditions were becoming unsafe, and they were getting chronically exhausted, making them prone to errors and lapses in security measures. The next thing I knew, I was studying prescription medication prices and health insurance premiums, or I was sitting with the world's greatest scientists, discovering that pollution kills millions of people every year. A day later, I might be meeting with a group of civil engineers who will describe how the state's thirteen thousand kilometres of levees are failing. I had no idea we had so many miles of levees— more than Holland or Louisiana. After my discussion with the engineers, I might meet with a group of nurses who wanted to explain why California hospitals needed a nurse-to-patient ratio greater than one to six. With one nurse for every six patients, it is very impossible for nurses to do all of their work in a single shift. For example, the average nurse can't lift a typical adult male on their own, so when that patient needs to get out of their hospital bed and go to the bathroom—a situation I witnessed first hand after my heart surgery in 2018—it sometimes takes two additional nurses, who are being pulled away from their other patients' work. I learned all of this from a single talk with a bunch of nurses!

It was fantastic. I was constantly learning. The more I learned and the more questions I asked of those who were educating me, the more I realised how everything was interconnected and how to become a great leader. Every day in Sacramento seemed like I was being given puzzle pieces to put together a mental model of how different systems functioned. And when I saw a picture of one of those systems that didn't make sense to me, or when the blueprint appeared to be broken, I realised it was time to act. I was fortunate. Even if I wasn't naturally inquisitive, as governor, I could demand people explain how the state functioned until it made sense to me, no matter how long it took. Most folks are not so fortunate. They lack the authority to demand that people explain the world to them, or they lack mentors like Fredi Gerstl to show them how to open their minds and absorb the world like a sponge. They must try to figure things out on their own, which may be very daunting and depressing without assistance. This, I believe, is one of the reasons why so many people are unhappy. They exist in a world they do not comprehend. The world is what it is, and people are who they are, and they must accept and cope with it. It's just their fate. Perhaps they were born into a life in which others were rich and they were poor, or others were tall, smart, or physically gifted and they were the polar opposite of those things—and no one explained to them that while some circumstances are unchangeable, others can be changed by being curious and a sponge, and then using the knowledge you gain to craft a vision for yourself.

In The Terminator, there's a famous line: "There's no fate but what we make for ourselves." Nobody has shown these poor creatures that they can control their own destiny. That they have the ability to drastically alter their circumstances, rendering the unchangeable things irrelevant. In fact, anyone can do it. Anyone can control their own destiny. You can do it, and you can start right now. Perhaps you have already done so by taking up this book. If that's the case, that's amazing. Now I want you to go out to someone in your life who hasn't begun working to improve their situation because they don't believe they can. It is critical that we reach out to those folks because curiosity is the first thing to die within someone who has been trained to believe that the world is what it is and that there is nothing they can do about it. When curiosity dies, the sponge that is their mind becomes a brittle brick that struggles to absorb new information and becomes extremely vulnerable when faced with difficult decisions. Do for them what Fredi Gerstl did for me and what I'm attempting to do for you with this book. More sponges are needed on the planet. It requires more bright, hopeful, driven, and useful people with vision. It needs people who can imagine the world of the future, which can only happen when people are able to absorb current world information.

Put Your Knowledge to Good Use

It's either use it or lose it. These words relate to so many aspects of life that they should be called a universal law.

If you don't use a muscle at the gym, it shrivels up and dies. A condition known as atrophy.

If you don't use your celebrity to undertake large projects or make a huge effect in Hollywood, your popularity will wane and your chance to accomplish either will disappear with it.

If you have money set aside for something in the government's annual budget and don't use it that year, it disappears the following year and you'll never see it again.

The rule with ripe fruit, political goodwill, media attention, coupons, economic opportunity, passing room on the highway, and other things is "use it or lose it." Most significantly, it applies to the knowledge you acquire throughout your life. If you don't exercise your mind like a muscle and put your knowledge to use on a regular basis, it will eventually lose its power.

One of the first occasions I saw the power of putting your expertise to use was during my three years as head of the President's Council on Physical Fitness and Sports, from 1990 to 1993. I visited schools in all fifty states as part of my duties working directly under President Bush. I visited with local officials to discuss policies. I delivered presentations in schools to excite students and persuade their parents to switch off the television and go outside. I moderated roundtables and panel discussions with educators, medical experts, fitness professionals, health-care leaders, nutritional experts, and anyone else I thought could help us fight childhood obesity and support physical education programs, which were being cut by states facing budget shortfalls. On these tours, I did a lot of talking, but I spent the majority of my time as a sponge, watching, listening, and asking questions to learn what was going on in the states from the people on the ground. What were their problems? What measures had they taken in order to save their physical education programs? What has been successful? What has gone wrong? What did they require? And why is this so?

I left every event with my head full of information, and for the time being, I had nowhere to put it except in the reports and recommendations that the council would provide each year. Then, in 1992, I met a fantastic man named Danny Hernandez, who headed the Inner-City Games (ICG) program out of the Hollenbeck Youth Center in East Los Angeles, approximately fifteen miles from my house.

Danny was born and raised in the rough neighbourhood of Boyle Heights in East Los Angeles. He graduated from high school there, went to college there after serving honourably in Vietnam, and continues to reside there to this day. He serves as the neighbourhood's eyes, ears, and heartbeat. And he'd noticed throughout the years that the summer, when school wasn't in session, was when the kids in his area were most prone to drugs and gang violence, because they didn't have anywhere to go or anything constructive to do every day. So, in 1991, he founded the ICG, an Olympic-style athletic and academic competition for children in East Los Angeles, in order to get them off the streets.

Danny and I met in the aftermath of the Los Angeles riots. The acquittal of four Los Angeles police officers that spring for the a year earlier roadside beating of Rodney King had sparked racial tensions in the city. Protests over the ruling sparked a week of extensive looting, arson, violence, and property destruction, primarily in poorer communities like Danny's. Stores, residential complexes, strip malls, and sometimes entire blocks were destroyed by fire. Danny had a feeling that the upcoming summer, which was just a month away, would be pivotal for the kids not only in Boyle Heights but throughout Los Angeles. If community leaders weren't paying attention, if they didn't have their ear to the ground as 500,000 children aged five to eighteen flooded out of classrooms and into city streets, things might go very wrong very quickly for everyone. Danny's concept was to expand the Inner-City Games beyond East Los Angeles to include kids from all over the city, and he was searching for aid from local politicians and celebrities to raise awareness and funds for the games.

That's when I entered the picture. Danny showed me around the Hollenbeck Youth Center. It had a gym, a boxing ring, and a plethora of sports equipment. There was a shower facility in the locker room. It provided quiet areas for homework and adult mentors on hand for assistance. It even featured a computer area with several machines, which was unheard of in 1992. Except for the computers, the space reminded me of the Graz gymnasium—it was a haven full of possibilities.

I took it all in as Danny told me about the work he'd been doing over the last decade and answered my many questions about the Inner-City Games. I believed that the more I learned, the better able I would be to assist, and I was eager to learn about this location and Danny's objective.

I was particularly curious as to why there were no other applications like his. I'd visited schools in nearly every state by this point, and I'd never seen or heard of anything like the Inner-City Games. Danny told me that obtaining state and federal monies had always been difficult for him, so that was probably why. It was also the reason he was talking to me about his program rather than the mayor or governor.

Danny was outstanding. His desire for the centre and the Olympics reminded me a lot of my early desires in bodybuilding and in Hollywood. We both had dreams that many people probably thought were insane, but if you could see what we saw and how much work we were prepared to put in to make those dreams a reality, you'd realise they weren't so crazy after all.

I'd had enough of hearing. I consented to participate. As the Games Executive Commissioner, I joined to assist Danny in expanding the ICG to Greater Los Angeles. We swiftly established the Inner-City Games Foundation as a non-profit organisation, and I spent the remainder of the summer informing and requesting money from friends and Hollywood bigwigs, while Danny secured corporate sponsorships. We weren't able to run the Games in time for summer break because the city was still recovering from the riots, but later that fall, the ICG hosted 100,000 local kids at various venues throughout Los Angeles as they competed in more than a dozen different athletic events, as well as essay, dance, and art contests where they could win scholarships. There was also a free career fair and health and fitness exams for children and their families.

It was a smashing success. Our efforts received a great deal of attention, which is precisely what you need when attempting to sell a concept like this to a metropolis the size of Los Angeles. The Games in '92 also received national media coverage, which was even better because it allowed Danny and me to fill the ICG bucket in the same way I had in the past for bodybuilding and my films. We were able to promote the ICG message on our terms, which drew in community organisers from other places, such as Atlanta and Chicago, who'd heard about Danny's work the year before and wanted to see it for themselves, to see whether it could work in their cities.

I couldn't say whether or not the ICG would be useful to those cities. What I did know for certain after my years as fitness czar is that each of those communities, and many more, required a program like this because they had the same issue Los Angeles was dealing with: every summer, hundreds of thousands of youngsters had nowhere to be and no one watching after them.

But I was also aware of something else. Cities were dealing with more than simply a summer issue. This was also a daily after-school issue. On my tour of America's schools, I'd begun to notice and hear about it. At the end of a school day, I would note that some kids got picked up by parents, while others swarmed aboard buses, but a lot of kids didn't do either. They lingered and laughed, or they dispersed in tiny groups to who knows where. I watched this pattern recur over and over again, especially at middle schools, which don't have the same kind of extracurricular athletics as high schools have. I was wondering if there was an explanation for what I was witnessing, so I asked the teachers and principals about it. They said that up to 70% of their students had parents who were either not present or who worked but couldn't afford daycare, leaving the children home alone after school, essentially unattended until their parents returned home from work. I also discovered from the police chiefs in those places that they referred to the time between the end of the school day and the end of the work day—approximately 3:00 to 6:00 p.m.—as "the danger zone," when teenagers were most prone to drugs and alcohol, to gangs and crime, and to teen pregnancy.

With the success of the Inner-City Games in the fall of 1992 and then again in the summer of 1993, I saw an opportunity to help Danny Hernandez extend the ICG beyond Los Angeles and to take it nationwide. My ambition was that ultimately, with adequate support and financing, we could expand its mission beyond the Games in the summer to include a year-round after-school program. I had more than hope, though. I had a vision for this, and I believed I had the expertise and capability to make it real. This was an assignment where I could finally take advantage of all the name recognition I'd acquired over the preceding two decades. I could employ all the relationships I'd made throughout that period. I could contact every politician, government official, and subject-matter expert I'd encountered throughout my tour of all fifty states as fitness czar. I could exploit every bit of information I had acquired from the panels and roundtables and Q&As and town halls I'd attended, from Anchorage to Atlanta. Like the sponge Fredi Gerstl trained me to be, I'd soaked up so much essential information, and now it was time to wring it all out for at-risk kids across the country.

I am a strike-while-the-iron-is-hot sort of guy, so together with a powerhouse of a woman named Bonnie Reiss, we cranked up a lobbying and fundraising machine as quickly as we could, and we hit the road. We flew to places all throughout America that we thought might benefit a program like the Inner-City Games and the more sophisticated version of it that we were intending to build out. On my own cash, using my own plane, we flew everywhere and lobbied any city and state politician who would sit down with us. We listened to them express their problems, many of which were related to raising funds to support our program throughout their city or even just one of their schools. I took all of that knowledge and assimilated it into my understanding of the wider challenges we were attempting to tackle, just as I did during my time on the President's Council. Then, through the ICG Foundation, we brought all of our knowledge to bear in giving answers to these cities, working with Bonnie and Danny, benefactors in our network, and state and federal organisations.

As a result, the ICG expanded steadily over the next few years to nine chapters around the country. Simultaneously, we began to expand into a year-round, school-based program called After-School All-Stars, which now serves approximately 100,000 children every day in over 450 schools across 40 American cities. It's a program that I'm still really proud to be a part of because it's a bright example of what's possible when you close your mouth and open your thoughts. When you take the time to listen and learn, and when you approach a situation with genuine compassion. When you offer everything you have to make your little part of the world a better place.

Curiosity. A thirst for knowledge. Being receptive to new ideas. Making use of your knowledge.

This, it turns out, is a recipe for anyone to effect genuine, significant change in the world, whether on a personal, professional, or governmental level. It's also how you bring about change in your circumstances and make room for a vision to grow and evolve, which is critical since I know you want to grow and evolve as well.

CHAPTER 7

BREAK YOUR MIRRORS

I follow a rule. You can call me Schnitzel, Termie, Arnie, or Schwarzie, but you should never call myself a self-made guy.

When I was younger and my written English comprehension abilities weren't as good as they are today, people called me that constantly perplexed me. Is he a self-made man? I knew it was a praise, but I couldn't help but wonder what these individuals were talking about. What about my family? They practically built me. So, how about Joe Weider? He transported me to America and made my childhood aspirations come true. What about Reg Park and Steve Reeves? They enabled me to have a realistic dream of transitioning from bodybuilding to acting. So, how about John Milius? He turned me into Conan the Barbarian.

I may have been overly precise in my interpretation of the term "self-made," but I never thought of myself as a self-made man. I saw myself as an example of the American Dream coming true. I felt (and continue to believe) that anyone could accomplish what I achieved. But, if anything, I felt like I was the polar opposite of a self-made man. Let's think about this for a moment. If I am an example of what is achievable in America, how can I claim to be self-made, given that I needed America to achieve any of my successes? Before I picked up my first barbell, I was indebted to the existence of an entire country!

As I grew older and learned more about the depth and history of the self-made man, I realised that what people were really trying to do was commend me on being diligent, focused, determined, and dedicated—all of the qualities required to achieve your goals. Of course, they were correct. All of those things applied to me. Nobody lifted the weights, said the lines, or signed the checks for me. However, this does not imply that I was self-made. Who I am, where I am, why I am here, and what I have accomplished are all the result of the influence of hundreds of unique people in my life.

I'm not the only one that feels this way. We are all here because of the contributions of others. Even if you've never had a positive impact in your life; even if everyone you've ever encountered was an impediment or an enemy, or if all they did was hurt you—they've all taught you something. You are a survivor. That you're better than that, that you're better than them. They demonstrated what not to do and who not to be. You're reading this book right now, attempting to better yourself because of the people in your life—for better or worse.

When you think about it, none of us have ever done anything on our own. We've always had assistance or direction. Others, whether we were conscious of it or not, had paved or marked the road for us in some way. And now that you know this, it's critical that you understand your obligation to give back. To assist others. To lower the ladder and raise the following group. Paying it forward. Being beneficial.

And let me tell you something: completely accepting that duty will change your life and the lives of many others. You'll wonder why you didn't notice this sooner. What began as a chore will rapidly become a privilege that you will never want to give up and will never take for granted.

Everyone Benefits from Giving Back

A book like this one is a dialogue between the author and the reader. Both of us. It's not me speaking to the entire world; it's me speaking to you. In my perspective, it is a meaningful and sacred bond. But something strange happens occasionally with books like this, when the author's purpose is to inspire you, the reader, to build a vision for your life, to think big, and to do whatever it takes to realise that vision. These novels have the potential to become permission slips for selfishness. They can be used to justify a "me against the world" mentality that makes self-improvement a zero-sum game. Someone has to become poorer in order for you to become richer. Someone must become weaker in order for you to get stronger. Everyone else must lose in order for you to win.

Outside of actual sports competition, let me tell you, it's almost all nonsense. Life isn't a zero-sum game. We can all grow, get richer, and become stronger together. Everyone has the ability to win, at their own time and in their own way.

That is accomplished by concentrating on all the ways we may give back to the people in our lives, whether they are our family, friends, neighbours, colleagues, or simply our fellow humans who breathe the same air we do. How can we assist them in realising their own goals? How can we help them achieve their objectives? What can we do to help them improve at the activities they enjoy? What can we do to help those in need? As you answer each of these questions for yourself in your personal relationships, you will discover that you will receive precisely what you offer.

This was strongest for me in the gym with my workout partners. We were always pushing each other. We discussed training methods and nutritional advice. We encouraged one another, but we also practically sat for one another while we lifted to failure or to our maximum weight. We all knew we'd be fighting against each other someday, so it wasn't like we weren't aware that each of us was helping our competitors grow better, but we also knew that if our training partners became stronger, it meant they could push us harder, which meant we could get stronger.

Helping one another out like that benefited not only us as individual bodybuilders, but also the sport of bodybuilding. I was the face of world bodybuilding in the 1970s, but if I had been up onstage with competitors who were orders of magnitude less muscular or defined than I was, I would have been just a curiosity, and bodybuilding would have seemed like nothing more than a circus sideshow. And who knows if I would have progressed to the same level. I'm not sure whether I would have gotten the body I did for each of my Mr. Olympia championships if Franco Columbu hadn't pushed me as a training partner or if Frank Zane hadn't stayed with me for a few months and shown me his tactics for getting more definition. Bodybuilding achieved such heights because a large group of us trained in the same gyms and helped one another improve, which improved competitions and grew the sport.

In movies, I witnessed the same positive feedback loop. Hollywood is replete with insecure actors who, if not properly guided or supported by their inner circle, will transform a film into a zero-sum struggle. They will aim to dominate every scene in which they appear, get more screen time than their co-stars, and blast other performers off the screen. They believe that this is what great actors do. This is how you become famous or win prizes. The reality is that such personal ambition and self-centred behaviour degrades movies. It makes people uncomfortable and has a detrimental impact on the watching experience. However, when performers assist one another in their scenes, when they set one another up, when they create room for one another to have amazing moments and memorable performances, that is when movies go from good to great and connect more deeply with audiences. That is when they achieve success. And having a successful film implies that the performers who were in it are more likely to get offers for bigger, more lucrative films than the one they just finished.

By being selfless, by assisting your coworker, competition, or colleague, you have the capacity to improve everyone's life and to create a great environment in which you can prosper and find happiness. This is why we enjoy television shows with large ensemble casts. That is why we respect firms like Patagonia, which prioritise consumers and employees before profits. It's why we appreciate great sports teams like the 2017 Golden State Warriors or the incredible Spanish national soccer teams: they're brilliant passers of the ball who play a team game that engages everyone and improves everyone.

On the other hand, this explains why we have such mixed views about selfish great sportsmen, arrogant CEOs, and narcissistic politicians. They almost never improve the lives of others. Even when they're "on our team," we only tolerate them if they're winning. We want to trade, fire, or vote them out of office the moment they start losing or things start going wrong. Because what's the sense of putting up with a selfish jerk who only thinks about themselves?

However, you do not have to be following a goal or a grand vision to reap the rewards of assisting others. There is a lot of science that shows that the simple act of giving back considerably boosts the giver's happiness, and that the rise occurs virtually instantly. In 2008, Harvard researchers conducted an experiment in which they offered one set of volunteers $5 and another group $20 and told them to spend it on themselves or give it away. When the researchers checked in with the participants at the end of the day, they discovered that those who gave their money away had a considerably better day than those who kept their money.

And here's the really intriguing part: there was no discernible difference in the level of improved enjoyment between persons who gave away $5 and those who gave away $20. It's not like the ones who gave away twenty dollars felt four times as happy as those who didn't. That is, it is not the amount that you contribute, but the fact that you give at all. The act of giving is what causes the heightened happiness.

Consider this: with the same act of compassion and generosity, you can make someone else's day as well as your own. And you don't have to be wealthy or wealthy to do it.

How to Give Back

It's easy for someone like me to sit here and tell you how important it is to give back or how good it feels to help others, with all of my life experience and resources at my disposal. But I understand that the benefits aren't always clear when you're young and penniless and trying to figure out what you want out of life. I also understand that it's not so easy when you're older and working multiple jobs, have a lot of mouths to feed, or spend every waking hour thinking about your own problems.

There may appear to be no time in your calendar for charitable contributions. When you do find time, your head has been down for so long trying to grind, or provide, or make your vision a reality, that it might be daunting to figure out how to best use that time, or whether your time is even important to someone else.

You start asking yourself questions such as, "Who am I? "I'm just a nobody trying to make ends meet." "What can I do?" I don't have any unique abilities." "What can I offer you?" I'm not as wealthy or famous as these other people."

The first thing to grasp is that, at its most basic, you do not need to restructure your life to aid others. All you have to do is keep your eyes and ears alert and your mind engaged with the world around you. Stop and give someone a hand or a hug if you see them struggling with a bag of groceries or a difficult mood. Answer the phone if a friend you haven't spoken to in years rings in the middle of the night. If you see someone who appears to be in need of assistance, whether they requested it or not, respond to the call. Reduce their load, even if only for five minutes or fifty feet. Helping others is a basic habit that involves only awareness, willingness, and a small amount of work. Without actively pursuing it, simply being aware of your surroundings will provide you with opportunities to assist others every day. And believe me when I say it will make you feel fantastic.

The second realisation is that you have more to contribute than you realise. I know you have the time, for example. If we looked at your entire twenty-four-hour day, I bet you have an hour to spare at least once or twice a week. Do you have any foreign language skills? Do you excel at maths? Do you have any reading skills? You may tutor middle-school students once a week at a nearby after-school program. You may read to elementary school pupils or patients at the children's hospital. Do you own a dependable automobile or van? You may deliver meals to the elderly or drive residents of nursing homes to physical therapy appointments. Do you have any handy skills? Do you have any tools? You may assist in repairing sports fields in your community before the season begins.

In terms of talents, it doesn't even have to get that complicated. Can you walk while also purchasing a carton of huge waste bags? David Sedaris, the great American author, has been cleaning up litter along the roads near his residence in the English countryside as part of his daily morning walks for so long that the county named a garbage truck after him, and Queen Elizabeth once invited him to Buckingham Palace for tea.

You don't need a great house to be motivated to pick up trash in your community. You don't need a house at all. Todd Olin, a homeless guy in West Los Angeles, became a local legend for cleaning up the streets of his Westchester area for hours every day for years. He removed trash, weeds, scrubbed graffiti, and cleaned drains and sewage grates. And he began with little more than a few grocery carts and a cheap plastic trash picker.

Giving back does not have to be done on a daily basis. In 2020, Lily Messing, a sixteen-year-old high school student from Tucson, Arizona, founded the 100+ Teens Who Care Tucson club, which meets just four times a year. Each member of the group, which is composed of high school students, pledges $25 each quarter (for a total of $100 for the year), after which they pick a local nonprofit in need of assistance, combine their funds for that quarter, and donate it directly to the organisation. They've given more than $25,000 to organisations that help local children, animals, domestic-abuse victims, and the homeless since 2020. $25 each year, four times a year. That's all it took to make such an impression!

If you're still struggling to think of ways to give back, take a personal inventory of what others have done for you in your life and try to pay it forward by doing the same things for others who may be in a similar circumstance. Get engaged in young soccer if you had a terrific soccer coach when you were a kid. If you received a scholarship from a local service group that assisted you in attending college, contact that organisation to see how you can give to their scholarship fund for the current crop of high school seniors. One of the things I do to repay Joe Weider's generosity in bringing me to America is to identify ambitious foreign citizens with big, worthy dreams and sponsor them for visas and green cards by writing letters on their behalf using my personalised stationery with the California governor's seal at the top. You don't have to be connected or creative to give back; all you need to do is think about it.

We discussed a lot in the previous chapter about how being curious, being a sponge, and asking smart questions are all strategies for opening your mind to the world's possibilities. They are also tools for opening your heart to its challenges and the ways you might contribute to their resolution. Sometimes the difficulties are minor, affecting only one person who requires immediate assistance. Other times, the problems are vast, chronic, or systemic, and assisting in their resolution becomes a cause to which you give back, like it did for Lily Messing, or it becomes part of your life's mission, as it did for Danny Hernandez and Mary Shenouda.

You can, of course, do both. Every day, I send a newsletter to hundreds of thousands of individuals to encourage them to be healthy and fit. It is, in many ways, a continuation and evolution of my work as fitness czar combating obesity in the early 1990s. At the same time, I get an equal amount of satisfaction from randomly spending ten minutes in the gym with some old geezer to show him good pulldown form, or talking to a seventeen-year-old kid who wants to start his own roofing business.

In either event, whether you've helped hundreds of people with your work or transformed one person's life with your words of wisdom, you'll have given back in the most meaningful way possible because you'll have altered the world. If you're still unsure about what you have to offer, simply be present and concentrate on the details. Little things have a way of growing into huge things, and I am convinced that one day something tiny will lead you to something big that you will feel equipped to give back to in a bigger way.

This is frequently the case for children aspiring to be Eagle Scouts, the highest rank in the Boy Scouts program. The final step toward becoming an Eagle Scout is to complete a service project that has a substantial influence on the community. Essentially, individuals must devise their own method of giving back. Most of these students figure out what they want their service project to be in a short amount of time since they've been connected with their communities for years, ready to respond to people in need.

Perhaps they are constantly assisting people in lifting shopping carts or baby carriages onto the sidewalk because the curbs in their town are too high, so for their project, they decide to pull permits, raise funds from local businesses, and hire a local contractor to help repair road surfaces and build handicap-accessible curb ramps all over town.

Perhaps they are always assisting neighbours in their search for their dogs, which keep fleeing from a park near their house due to the park's outdated and deteriorating fence. So they decide to remodel and repair the fencing with the help of some of their fellow Scouts, using donated materials from the local hardware store, and then petition the city council to have the place legally classified as a dog park, ensuring that future maintenance is taken care of.

There are a thousand different variations of this Eagle Scout narrative, but the best part is that there are a million different ways you may apply the lesson at the heart of them to use your time, abilities, and resources for the benefit of others. And, in my experience, once you start, it's difficult to stop.

Giving Back Becomes an Addiction

My first structured experience with giving back occurred in the late 1970s, when I was invited to help coach Special Olympics participants in powerlifting at a university in Wisconsin's northwest corner. I worked with groups of teenage boys with varying degrees of intellectual disability for two or three days as part of a study to explore if lifting weights could be safe for them as athletes and effective as a therapeutic tool. The whole thing was incredible, but it was our first day together, concentrated on the bench press, that I remember in vivid detail even now.

I recall the kids being cautious and withdrawn at first. I recall flexing and posing for them and allowing them to squeeze my biceps or poke my chest to entice them out of their shells. I recall how nice it felt to earn their trust and see their excitement increase as they lay down on the bench and positioned themselves under the bar for the first time in their life. I recall a few of them struggling. It was a little frightening to see the bar immediately above their heads and then feel gravity bring the weight down on them through their hands. It was probably as strange to those kids as it was to me to be educating and speaking with them. But I recall thinking that if they had the guts and strength to face their worries and try something new, I couldn't let my doubt get in the way and maybe disappoint them. Instead, I attempted to equal their warmth, passion, and openness. I recall that at the end of the day, each kid had completed many sets of bench press. Even the most fearful of the boys I got under the bar and banged off some reps, including one boy who panicked and started crying until I calmed him down by standing him next to me and designating him my official rep counter.

I'll never forget that kid. After assisting me in counting reps for some of the other guys, I could tell he was becoming more at ease with the weights. He'd seen them lift the weight and it hadn't crushed them. I asked him if he wanted to try again, and he responded yes. His pals were ecstatic for him. I stepped behind him and slowly placed the bar in his hands while he laid down on the bench with his head between the vertical bar supports.

"Now give me ten reps," I instructed. He knocked them out like they didn't exist. His pals went crazy for him. A barbell-sized smile spread across his face. "I think you're ready for more weight," that's what I stated.

Each side received a ten-pound plate. "Try to give me three reps," I said. His pals encouraged him. He took a big breath and expelled them with little effort.

"Wow, you're so strong," I exclaimed. "I believe I will face competition soon." "Are you capable of doing more?"

He excitedly nodded. Two extra ten-pound plates were added. He then did three more reps. Within an hour and a half, this youngster had progressed from being scared of the barbell to lifting 85 pounds three times without help. He rose from the bench, I gave him a high-five, and his friends surrounded him.

I was thrilled with a spiritual joy as I stood there watching these young guys celebrate their friend's accomplishment. It was so overwhelming that I became perplexed. I had made no money. This was not a career-advancing move. Doing stuff like this wasn't really part of my bigger picture at the time. And, to be honest, I didn't feel like I was putting in much effort or making any sacrifices. So, what made me so happy?

I understood it was because I had assisted these children. I'd transformed this boy's life by doing something as easy as turning there, being helpful and encouraging, and teaching a few things. He now had confirmation that he could do it, that he was powerful enough to do more than simply lift weights. I'd taught him something about himself that he might carry with him into new, uncomfortable, and frightening situations for the rest of his life. He'd never be the same again after that day. Neither of them were his pals. I wasn't either.

It turns out that there was a lot in this experience for me, just not in the way I'd previously measured things. I was able to use my knowledge and expertise to assist this group of young people who were less fortunate than me in becoming better at something, becoming stronger, more confident, and feeling better about themselves. I'd given back for no other reason than that they needed help and someone had asked me.

I knew I wanted to do more of it right away. If you were in my shoes, you would have felt the same way. But don't take it from me. Consider science. Over the last four decades, psychologists and neuroscientists have discovered that giving back, whether through charity donations or volunteering, causes the production of oxytocin and endorphins. These are the same hormones produced by your brain during sex and exercise. Giving back is also known to produce vasopressin, a neurochemical related with love. In fact, just thinking about or remembering altruistic moments causes the release of these same hormones.

This phenomenon is known to social scientists as "helper's high." That is the power of giving back. It's a natural high with highly addictive characteristics. I know all of this now, but for months and years after my weekend in Wisconsin, I was just looking for the oxytocin and endorphin high like an addict chasing the dragon.

As a result of our collaboration, university researchers and Special Olympics officials discovered that weight lifting offered the youngsters more confidence than nearly any other sport they tried. The impact was so substantial that they asked for my assistance in designing a powerlifting competition for the Special Olympics

Games and determining which lifts should be included. I jumped at the opportunity. We chose to begin with the bench press and deadlift because they are the most basic movements and put children with balance concerns or motor coordination deficits in the least amount of danger. They're also the most exciting to watch and participate in because they entail the most weight being lifted. After assisting in the design of the curriculum, I worked with groups of children in a number of other places around the country before becoming an official International Trainer. Within a few years, powerlifting would be included at regional Special Olympics tournaments around the United States, and it would eventually become a fixture at the International Games, where it remains one of the most popular sports among both athletes and fans. I still enjoy cheering on those brave men and women at every Special Olympics Games, and I'm overjoyed that my daughter and son-in-law have joined the cause as worldwide ambassadors.

Later, President Bush asked me to chair the President's Council on Physical Fitness and Sports because of my work with the Special Olympics. I was as busy and in demand as I'd ever been at the moment. I was making two movies a year and handled all of the foreign promotion for them. I was earning $20 million every film. But the joy I felt from pumping up those Special Olympics kids was greater than any feeling I'd ever had walking a red carpet, and it was more valuable to me than another big payday, so the opportunity to replicate that feeling by helping even more kids, including some of the country's most vulnerable schoolchildren, was a no-brainer. I answered yes right away and committed to travelling on my own cash, flying my own plane, and paying for everyone's food and lodging during our tour of all fifty states.

My expanding duties with the Special Olympics and the President's Council took up a lot of my free time, but not so much that I stopped exploring for new ways to give back. I was sucked in. I have no doubt that helper's high played a significant role in bringing Danny Hernandez and me in the same room for the first time in 1992. I know it was a huge part of pushing to expand the Inner-City Games to other cities over the next decade and to expand its mission into a year-round after-school program across the country.

This is what happens when you get hooked on giving back. Like a drug, you want to do more of it, but you also want to go bigger. You want to assist more people, more frequently, and with more things. For me, that eventually meant giving up my big movie paychecks, running for governor of California and refusing the taxpayer-funded salary, and then shifting my focus to the Schwarzenegger Institute at USC and the Schwarzenegger Climate Initiative, where our goals of reforming our political system to shift power from politicians to the people and ending pollution have the potential to help hundreds of millions, if not billions, of people.

Every day, I wake up thinking about these things, which give me a tremendous sense of purpose. That same feeling is available to you, to everyone, once you take the initial step toward giving back and allowing endorphins to flow through your veins.

Shatter the Glass

It's fascinating to reflect on the forty-plus years since that journey to Wisconsin and see how my vision has developed as my objectives have shifted. At first, I was entirely focused on myself, and my vision included professional achievement as well as personal fame and money. That vision informed all of my decisions, and the amount to which I felt glad to serve others was largely determined by how it fit into that goal. But as time passed and giving back became a bigger part of my life, the dial began to shift toward us. Helping others made me happy not because it advanced my personal aims, but because it was my personal goal. It was no longer a means to an end, but rather an end in itself.

Making giving back a priority in my life was confirmed for me shortly after my tenure on the President's Council, during a speech delivered to the Yale University graduating class by my late father-in-law, Sargent Shriver. Sarge, as his friends called him, was thoughtful, polite, and bright. He led from the heart like no one else I've ever met. He genuinely cared about others, and he put his money (and time) where his mouth was.

Sarge established the Peace Corps, Head Start, VISTA (Volunteers in Service to America), Job Corps, Upward Bound, and a variety of other philanthropic organisations that assisted neglected communities in the United States and around the world. In addition to her other efforts in support of persons with intellectual disabilities, he was the chairman of the board of the Special Olympics, which his wife, Eunice, created. It's not an exaggeration to say that the Shrivers dedicated their whole adult lives to helping others.

Sargent was in his late eighties when he delivered his Yale Day lecture. He'd seen and done a lot in his life. He was full of wisdom that he wanted to impart with the next generation of leaders about having the ability to change the world into anything they want. He did, however, provide some counsel.

He exclaimed, "Break your mirrors!" "Yes, shatter the glass." In our self-absorbed world, begin to look less at yourself and more at each other. Learn more about your neighbour's face and less about your own. When you're thirty, forty, fifty, or even seventy years old, counting your friends will bring you more satisfaction and contentment than counting your dollars. You'll gain more joy from having enhanced your neighbourhood, town, state, country, and fellow human beings than you would from your muscles, figure, automobile, house, or credit rating. Being a peacemaker will benefit you more than being a warrior. "Shatter the mirrors."

Sargent delivered his speech in 1994, over thirty years ago. Do you think his message is still as relevant today as it was then? I feel it will be just as significant for future generations. I say this knowing that advice like Sargent's frequently appears to come from elites who prefer to talk about saving the world while relaxing in the comfort and safety of their yacht or walled vacation home.

"Easy for him to say," you may think to yourself.

What you must realise is that Sargent was not suggesting that personal aspiration had no worth or satisfaction. He recognized that, while having muscles isn't the most important thing in the world, having a strong, healthy physique is beneficial and necessary for living a long life. He understood that owning a nice car that drives smoothly and on which you can rely relieves you of one concern. He knew that having a large enough house that can accommodate your entire family and feels like home can be a source of tremendous pride.

Giving back, according to Sargent, is a source of greater contentment, in part because it puts personal goals in the correct perspective. I would even go so far as to say that breaking your mirrors and taking care of all those people behind the glass who could use your help is not only a greater source of happiness, but it also makes the things you want for yourself more meaningful and precious.

That all sounds very academic, I know, but I saw it in action when I was governor during the fire season. Every year, between June and October, I would visit firefighters as they rested between twelve- to eighteen-hour shifts battling fast-moving walls of flames in extreme heat and dangerous conditions in an effort to save homes and lives. I could tell they were fatigued from travelling in and out of valleys, chopping down trees and building firebreaks, and when I asked them how they were feeling, they were as humble as their deeds were heroic. But what struck me the most was that on more than one occasion, I'd be speaking with a local firefighter who was on the front lines while their own house was potentially on fire. Everything they owned, their prized possessions, the home where they were raising a family—all of it could have gone up in flames at any moment, and these firefighters hadn't given a second thought to whether or not their proper place was back at home trying to save their own homes or out on the fire line helping their neighbours.

Forget about shattering their mirrors; these were the types of folks who didn't have mirrors in the first place. They were continuously on the lookout for others. Giving back and assisting others is exactly what they did. They were completely focused on us, and I've looked up to them as role models in selflessness and sacrifice ever since. I believe we all should. I doubt many of us can achieve that level of selflessness, but we can strive for it.

In my case, I would say that my life is primarily we-focused these days, and the only reason any of it is me-focused is so that I can keep producing money to fund all of the we-focused things I care about. The ability to send a million dollars to the First Responders Fund in

March 2020, for example, was the result of continuing to focus on personal goals and knowing that there will always be money to give back and help solve big, urgent problems that are being bungled by politicians who don't care about helping others.

I'm not telling you these stories to encourage you to do what I did or what firefighters, commandos, and first responders do. I'm also not asking you to become Robin Hood or Mother Teresa, or to give up your personal ambitions or things. I'm merely asking you to break your mirrors and do what you can for others. I'm asking you to return the favour. Paying it forward. To be as useful as possible. And I'm asking you to do it for the same reason any of us has chosen to give back. Because we owe a debt of appreciation to those who have helped us get to where we are today. Because we have the ability to do for the next generation what the previous generation did for us. Because it will benefit the entire world. Because it will make you happier in ways you never expected.

When you've lived long enough and worked hard enough to see your wildest goals come true, you realise that we're all connected. We're all in this together, this thing called life. This isn't a zero-sum game. It has the potential for several winners. There are an infinite number of victors... as long as you make giving back part of the game rules. We all benefit when we give back a way of life, when we break down our mirrors to see all the folks behind the glass who could use our support.

It makes no difference how young or old you are, how much or how little you have, how much you've done or how much remains to be done. Giving more will always bring you more. Do you want to help yourself? Assist others. Learn to begin from there, and you will become the most beneficial version of yourself—to your family, friends, neighbourhood, nation... and the world.

The contents of this book may not be copied, reproduced or transmitted without the express written permission of the author or publisher. Under no circumstances will the publisher or author be responsible or liable for any damages, compensation or monetary loss arising from the information contained in this book, whether directly or indirectly. .

Disclaimer Notice:

Although the author and publisher have made every effort to ensure the accuracy and completeness of the content, they do not, however, make any representations or warranties as to the accuracy, completeness, or reliability of the content. , suitability or availability of the information, products, services or related graphics contained in the book for any purpose. Readers are solely responsible for their use of the information contained in this book

Every effort has been made to make this book possible. If any omission or error has occurred unintentionally, the author and publisher will be happy to acknowledge it in upcoming versions.

Printed in Great Britain
by Amazon

35244751R00073